D1431381

RELUCTANT RESISTER

Jeff Dietrich

RELUCTANT RESISTER

UNICORN PRESS, INC.

The publisher would like to thank all the following for assistance in the publication of this book: Joan Trefacanty, Ann Davies and Teo Savory in the editorial preparation; Polly Potter and Rick Bruning in setting the type and laying out the pages; John Schuler and Bonny Dolman in printing the book; and all the members of the Los Angeles Catholic Worker Community, Unicorn Press, Universal Printing and Inter-Collegiate Press.

Unicorn Press, Inc.
P.O. Box 3307
Greensboro, North Carolina 27402

Library of Congress Cataloguing in Publication:

Dietrich, Jeff, 1948 -
Reluctant Resister

1. Dietrich, Jeff, 1948 -   . 2. Pacifists—United States—Correspondence.
3. Military Service, Compulsory—United States—Draft Resisters—Correspondence.
4. War—Religious aspects—Catholic Church.   I. Title.

JX1962.D53A4   1983   327.1′72′0924   82-19990

ISBN 0-87775-156-0
ISBN 0-87775-157-9 (pbk.)

ILLUSTRATIONS

A 32-page signature on glossy paper, between pages 24 and 25:

1) PHOTO BY ARDON ALGER of Jeff Dietrich circulating petitions in Anaheim prior to the 1979 Arms Bazaar
2) LEAFLET circulated prior to the 1979 Arms Bazaar
3) LEAFLET circulated prior to the 1979 Arms Bazaar
4) LEAFLET circulated prior to the 1979 Arms Bazaar
5) LEAFLET circulated prior to the 1979 Arms Bazaar
6) PHOTO BY ARDON ALGER of mass demonstration, October, 1979
7) PHOTO BY ARDON ALGER of mass demonstration, October, 1979
8) PHOTO BY MARTY BABAYCO of Buddhist monks, Bruce Genung and John Lundholm (LACW) in the background, far right, Rosemary Occhiogrosso (LACW)
9) PHOTO BY GARY VOTH of Kent Hoffman, with Rosemary Occhiogrosso at the right
10) PHOTO BY ARDON ALGER
11) PHOTO BY ARDON ALGER
12) PHOTO BY MARK SANDERS
13) PHOTO BY ARDON ALGER
14) PHOTO BY MARTY BABAYCO
15) PHOTO BY GARY VOTH

Folks for the Future

It was yet another typical day at the Los Angeles Catholic Worker: Catherine Morris breaking up a knife fight outside the soup kitchen; our nurse, Catherine Bax, rushing off to County Hospital with a man in diabetic shock.   I wasn't expecting any surprises.

Then, somewhere between chopping the onions and mincing the garlic, Jeff blurted out, "I suppose we should get arrested at the Anaheim Arms Bazaar."

My knife slipped, my jaw fell and my heart dropped to somewhere just this side of China.   Jeff's well-known reluctance in matters of political resistance is surpassed only by my utter panic.   His reluctance is to my terror what a sand box is to the Sahara Desert.   I don't like being arrested.

This was obviously not an easy proposition for me to hear.   "The Arms Bazaar is coming next month and I don't think we can let it come and go without some statement of our opposition."   Jeff's conviction made sense. It usually does.   Certainly it would be an abomination to allow this military showcase to come within a few miles of where we live without our voicing serious protest.   It was just that protest and arrest are often one and the same at the Catholic Worker in Los Angeles.   And I'm not one easily coaxed into investing my fear that deeply in an act of conscience.

That was 1978.   October.   And from that single conversation over the preparation of a meal for hundreds of men and women on L.A.'s Skid Row came the difficult decision to take a stand at the First Annual Military Electronics Exposition at the Anaheim Convention Center.   (The Military Electronics Exposition is a convention of international corporations each involved in the research, development and production of electronic military software—laser targeting systems, surveillance sensors, electronic weapon detonators, etc.   The exposition is an arena for the marketing of the most modern techniques for killing to over 3000 representatives of the military in the U.S. and around the world.)

A month later, in mid-November, Jeff and I were joined by Marty Babayco and Jon Allen as we stood in front of the doors at the Convention Center, a single banner in our hands, with the solitary statement: "No!" We were arrested, spent a night in jail, were harshly scolded in court the next day by Judge Robert Fitzgerald, and given a one-year probation. Judge Fitzgerald made it clear that he did not want, nor expect, to see us again.

Impure as it may appear, fear is a great motivator. The knowledge that the Arms Bazaar would certainly return in 1979 drove us to an all-out attempt to prevent its, and our, repeat performance in Anaheim. And so in early March of 1979, five members of the L.A. Catholic Worker (Debbie Garvey, Bruce Genung, Marisue Cody, Jon Allen and I) gathered together one evening to discuss plans for stopping the Arms Bazaar scheduled for October 23, 24 and 25 of that same year.

Our plans were simple enough; we would organize a support group in Orange County (where the city of Anaheim is located) that would broaden the base of opposition to the upcoming event. All of our efforts would be coordinated with the Alliance for Survival (an antinuclear organization in Los Angeles). Together we would gather a cross section of Orange County residents to focus on and confront an issue in their own back yard. This group would also lend a legitimacy that we did not have: middle-class, local residents, rather than "carpetbagging radicals" from Los Angeles.

A letter of invitation to over 400 Orange County subscribers to our two-penny newspaper, *The Catholic Agitator*, yielded an initial turnout of 40 people. That group, with a few exceptions, remained active and involved, taking on an identity and credibility quite different from our own.

To appear as nonthreatening and innocuous as possible, they chose the name Orange County Folks for the Future. Their agenda was two-fold: 1) attempt to stop the Military Electronics Exposition by every legal means possible (and in this, seek to raise the consciousness of the county residents about the wider implications of weapons technology and the arms race) and 2) if unable to keep the exposition from coming to Anaheim, then to collaborate with the Alliance for Survival in organizing a broad base, peaceful, legal protest by hundreds of local residents.

The first step meant creating a network of concern about the Arms Bazaar by: 1) publicizing the scheduled event via letters to the editor of all local Orange County newspapers; 2) organizing a letter writing campaign to the mayor of Anaheim; and 3) getting on the agenda to meet with the Anaheim city council, owner and manager of the Convention Center.

Unfortunately, only a few papers were willing to print letters about the military expo, but the mayor did receive hundreds of letters complaining about the event scheduled to be in his city. His response was to disregard the letters because a majority were written by nonresidents of Anaheim. If the people of his city were to voice their opposition, he declared in writing, then he might be forced to listen.

That was all that we needed to begin a massive petition drive. Anaheim had over 100,000 residents and we had only five weeks before we were scheduled to meet with the city council. Our hope was to go into the meeting with 5,000 signatures of Anaheim residents—all protesting the event to be held in their city.

Five weeks, several thousand petitioning hours and 7,000 signatures later, we walked into the city council chambers expecting to be given some credence in response to the serious "voice" we represented in opposition to the scheduled exposition. TV cameras stood waiting, the chamber room was filled to overflowing. Unfortunately, when the agenda item before ours, the hotly contested debate about "Bingo Night in Anaheim" was finished, all the media and 90% of those in attendance left the council chambers. Thirty-five of us remained and five were allowed to speak for three minutes each. The petitions were presented; the mayor excused himself for a dinner engagement; our speeches were made; the bland response of the council was unanimous; "We have no right to make 'political' decisions about the nature of events being held in our Convention Center." "But how," we asked, "could they so quickly dismiss the over 7,000 signatures we were presenting from local, voting residents?" "We have no way to evaluate their validity," came the council response. The stage had obviously been set for a method of protest beyond the legal means that we felt we had so thoroughly exhausted.

From that time on, the Orange County Folks for the Future, led by Karen Litfin, Ellie Cohen and Paul O'Connor, began coordinating with the Alliance for Survival the organizing of a massive peaceful, legal protest at the Military Electronics Exposition. Churches, peace groups, unions and colleges from throughout Los Angeles and Orange County were contracted to oppose the exposition. A candlelight vigil and rally were planned for the 22nd of October, the night before the Arms Bazaar was to open.

At the same time the L.A. Catholic Worker began a separate organizing campaign of its own, to gather together as many as possible to participate in civil disobedience. We published "An Open Invitation to Civil Disobedience" in our newspaper, which brought a steadily increasing response of people willing to be arrested. We scheduled, required and held a program in nonviolence and civil disobedience training for all of those planning to participate.

Two meetings were held with the Anaheim Police Department, in which we shared with them our intention of being arrested and our commitment to nonviolence. A police lieutenant was assigned to us as a liaison and a relationship of growing trust was established.

Press releases were issued; the media were given background information packets; a spokeswoman for our combined efforts with the Alliance and O.C. Folks for the Future was chosen. We were ready.

Finally on the night of October 22, over 2000 people gathered one mile from the Convention Center to begin their march. With full television and newspaper coverage, a two-hour candlelight vigil was held with musicians, prayer and the traditional rhetoric from speakers.

Over the next three days, in groups of from two to seven, 36 people were arrested. All were taken to Orange County Jail. Some were quickly released on their own recognizance; many elected to remain in jail until arraigned early the following week. On the fifth day following the last arrest, 21 men and women entered a court room in Fullerton, California and there pled guilty to charges of criminal trespass. (The remaining 15 were to plead "not guilty" in court trials and be found innocent.) Each of these was given a one-year probation and a jail sentence of five days (time served). Two, Jeff Dietrich and I, were sent back to county jail so that we might return to court the next day, once again to stand before Judge Robert Fitzgerald, the man who a year earlier had sentenced us to one day in jail and one year of probation. We had two weeks of that probation remaining.

It is here that the reader is introduced to the thought and experience recorded in the journal of *Reluctant Resister*. The flow of those events was, from its beginning, nothing short of miraculous on a daily basis for both Jeff and me. That miracle may best be summarized by the transformation which took place in the life of Robert Fitzgerald. The initial harshness of Judge Fitzgerald's sentence, his decision to double the jail time recommended by the district attorney, his personal remarks of contempt toward our purpose and method, all told us that here was one profoundly closed to who we were and what we were doing.

Two months later we stood before this judge, none of us, Jeff, Robert Fitzgerald or I, any longer the same. Each, in a different way, had been broken open by the difficulty, the darkness and unknowing of the last 59 days. Fifty-nine days! As I say it, I see it as an embarrassingly brief amount of time to warrant such statements about inner transformation. And yet, as I sat talking alone with Robert Fitzgerald in his private chambers eight days after our release, a definite difference was recognizable and openly admitted. He spoke of the confusion he experienced, of the influence provided by receiving over 700 letters of concern on our behalf, of the movement from distrust to appreciation for our sincerity and tenacity of commitment. He had gone through a rare agony for one so solidly entrenched in power and the pride of power. He had chosen to admit openly and publicly the mistake he had made.

It was here that I told him of a dream that I had experienced after my first month in jail. It was Christmas morning on Skid Row, we were serving our usual Christmas breakfast to 1200 people. As I stood dishing out large slices of ham to those passing before me, Robert Fitzgerald stood beside me serving great helpings of bread and coffee. There was a sense of ease about us, a peace both inner and outer that spoke of full reconciliation. I awoke crying. It was while listening to the telling of this dream that Robert Fitzgerald began to soften around the eyes, his voice relaxed, the tone even more open than it had been. In sadness he spoke of the life of one he loved very much, one who had lived out the last part of his life on Skid Row. He would, it seems, be honored to serve with me one day a special Christmas meal in that tiny kitchen in the heart of Los Angeles.

Kent Hoffman

The
Ammon Hennacy
House of Hospitality

The journals and letters that make up this volume record a pilgrim at point of crisis. They reveal a man reflecting upon action taken in the name of conviction and coming to new and deeper understanding of the meaning of that action and the consequences of accepting the role of prophet. They are, therefore, intensely personal.

Yet, because Jeff Dietrich has been for 11 years a member and, in many ways, a leader of a unique (albeit constantly changing) community of individuals—the Los Angeles Catholic Worker Community—united by certain common concerns, certain visions of what the world is and, more importantly, what it ought to be, these journals are also a reflection of that community and, as such, they can be best understood only in terms of a shared experience. The community, in turn, must be considered in the context of the larger Catholic Worker movement (of which the Los Angeles Worker is an independent but organically related part) and of the personalities of those whose temperaments, as much as their convictions, created and defined that movement.

Any attempt at describing the history or philosophy of a group of men and women living in extraordinary deviance from the assumptions and values of the culture around them, and doing so on the basis of ethical and religious conviction, runs the risk of rapidly degenerating into hagiography. As antidote to this subtle lure, it is well to remember Henry Miller's comment on the radical left of his youth, during the heady days of the Industrial Workers of the World and the Russian Revolution: "People who are always worrying about the state of the world, and how to change it, either don't have any personal problems to worry about or are refusing to face the problems they've got." To admit the truth in Miller's genial cynicism is not to invalidate the concerns and actions—often sacrificial actions—of those who devote themselves to the "state of the world." The fact that one seeks to live the truth from decidedly mixed motives (and with often mixed results) detracts neither from the truth nor the effort. In fact, from a Christian perspective, we have no reason to expect that our prophets will achieve any perfection of grace in this life. We serve a God relentless in choosing the foolishness—and presumably the fools—of this world to confound the wise, a God who reveals strength through human inadequacy.

The instinctual urge to paint halos must be resisted. Creating false icons encourages the objects of our idolatry in the pernicious gratifications of self-satisfaction and pharisaism—the twin hallmarks of both the religious right and left. It makes our heroes a special breed apart which can offer little in the way of model for the rest of us, since they are denied their full share in our common foibles and brokenness. It raises false expectations in other spiritual pilgrims seeking living exemplars of how we are to live and runs the risk that these expectations, once betrayed—as they inevitably must be—will leave bitterness and cynicism in their wake.

Yet the revisionist spirit, too enthusiastically embraced, is equally deadly. It can lead one to forget that—in a world where personal value is judged on power, productivity and the amassing of goods—any movement toward divestment and solidarity with the weak and exploited represents a high moral response. It can blind one to the fact that—in a society where "well adjusted" is the highest accolade and where adjustment is defined in terms of unthinking participation in a system categorically at odds with justice, the gospel of Christ and the survival of the race—even small, compromised steps in the direction of responsible discontinuity with that society must count as heroism.

The Catholic Worker movement has been marked by strong personalities, particularly those of Dorothy Day, Peter Maurin and Ammon Hennacy. Their personal pilgrimages and continuing processes of discovery have become—for hundreds of others in the movement—the stuff of what it means to be a Catholic Worker. In a voluntary association without rules, vows, credos or written constitutions, the force of personality inevitably assumes a dominance unmatched in most more conventional organizations. Yet Day and Maurin (and later Hennacy) did not operate in a spiritual, political or philosophical vacuum.

The roots of that organic aggregate which came to be the Worker "philosophy" can be traced to at least five primary springs: the Catholic (indeed, general Christian) teaching of the unity of human persons in the Mystical Body of Christ and the radical social teachings of Jesus in the Gospels;

the new vision for relationship between worker and labor, individual and group, proposed by the anarcho-syndicalist movement; the postwar French "Christian personalist" philosophers' understanding of the essential connection between personal salvation and the redemption of the cosmos (both being dependent upon the infusion of divine love into the process of history through individual decision); the cooperative, decentralist, agrarian social models found in the writings of the Russian utopian, Prince Kropotkin, and the English Catholic "distributist" thinkers (Chesterton, Belloc and McNabb); and, finally, the pacifist tradition of the historic peace churches of the radical reformation.

As for the Worker movement's roots in the Christian faith, Day, Maurin and their theological mentors recognized that at the base of all Christian teaching about the nature of redemption is the belief not only that God, in becoming a human person in Christ, "saves" women and men individually from the destruction of an unbridled ego attempting to be God unto itself (the fundamental meaning of "sin"), but that, in Christ, individual human beings are taken up into the loving unity of deity, they become part of Christ and therefore part of each other, members, now, not only of a common physical race, a common species, but of a new organism which has as its unifying principle—or, in Biblical terms, its spirit—the loving life of God. That organism is the Mystical Body of Christ. Thus, in the Incarnation, men and women are brought into radically deeper and more significant relationship to each other. Christ (and therefore God) is now potentially present to us in each other and what we do to each other is, unmistakably, what we do to Christ. In the context of this vision, the "radical" social teachings of Jesus (renunciation of worldly goods for the sake of others, turning the other cheek, giving one's coat to another in need, etc.) cease to be idealistic or visionary—they become immensely and immediately practical. What other response could one have to a family member, a part of one's own body, the presence of Christ?

Dorothy Day said that the truth of the Mystical Body of Christ lay behind everything that the Worker movement was and did. It was the faith from which specific action took its meaning, it was the reality out of which the social justice teachings of Jesus (and, later, of the church, through councils and popes) grew and, most importantly, it was a hope that made love—not sentimentality or feeling, but love as action, love for another real person in a given existential moment—the fundamental starting point of life itself. It was this vision that differentiated the Worker approach to the traditional "works of mercy"— feeding the hungry, clothing the naked, offering hospitality to the homeless— from those of conventional charity: it was no longer a matter of condescending (ultimately self-serving) legalism in which one doled out a tithe to the "unfortunate," it was a response of the self to family members, to the Head of the family Himself. It was this, as well, that differentiated the Worker from the conventional left, especially communism, with which it shared much in history and conviction. No individual, no encounter, could be viewed as a means to the revolutionary end, nor could struggle and conflict be the basic transaction for genuine change. Only self-giving love could measure up to the reality of the new relationship between persons in Christ.

Alongside their avowed Christian identity, both Day and Maurin referred to themselves as anarchists, a word which, through misuse, has lost nearly all meaning. The press, speaking on behalf of the system, convinced the world that all anarchists were bomb-toting terrorists. Too often, self-professed anarchists seemed to confuse anarchism with infantile megalomania—their right to do whatever they wanted, when they wanted, and everyone else's right to put up with it without complaint. But classic anarchism was not terrorism (terrorism was, in fact, antithetical to its principles), nor was it an argument for social chaos. Rather, it was a new vision for society in which the dignity of each individual, in each moment, was paramount and in which power, rather than being placed in the hands of a financial oligarchy (as in classic capitalism) or of an all-powerful state (as in classic communism) was entrusted to small voluntary collectives of workers (i.e., of those directly affected by the decisions of the group) who would arrive at decision through consensus and mutual toleration. Power, in a real sense, is thus swallowed up in service and the heresy shared by capitalism and communism—that the end justifies the means, that individuals are subordinate to ultimate goals (be those goals profit or the dictatorship of the proletariat)—is soundly rejected. Practically, then, there are no means, per se, every moment is an end in itself, every person an end in herself or himself. The revolution must work now, one on one, you on me, or it is no revolution worthy of the name. It does not take great imagination to see how this concept of anarchism, bonded to a deep understanding of the Mystical Body of Christ, would forge for Dorothy Day, Peter Maurin and others an at once demanding, yet liberating, new model for life in the world.

That bonding, that synthesis, found a natural vehicle in the "Christian personalist" philosophy developed in the writings of, among others, Nicolai Berdyaev, Dostoevsky and Jacques Maritain. Personalism, as it came to be understood in the Catholic Worker movement, took the immediacy of anarchistic revolution—each moment is the revolution, each individual the focus of liberation—and shot it through with the Christian vision of the Mystical Body—each moment is the Kingdom of God, each individual the presence of Christ—to arrive at a call, an "agenda" for life action. To be a personalist was to accept the call, to recognize the need to internalize the revolution/Kingdom, to actualize it in the moment, at once, without waiting for the world to catch up, without struggling to change institutions, even to change others (at least at first). The call was to drop everything and change oneself, to start living as if (and in the assurance that) the Kingdom of God was indeed present (whether anybody else knew it or not), to live as if Christ truly did confront one, moment by moment, in other persons (especially in their need), to live as if the revolution (in its deepest sense) were here. That change, that new kind of living, would be grounded in and infused with the life-force of the Mystical Body itself: divine love. Loving action, taken as an inescapable personal imperative, became the supreme guide and basis for living. It was the pearl of great price for which a man sells all that he has. For the personalist, the fact that the world at large does not recognize the Kingdom of God in its midst, does not see Christ in the least of these his brothers and sisters (and, for that matter, the greatest—true personalism allows no comforting "us-them" dichotomies), the fact that the world fights the revolution with all the means of power and convention, can only mean one thing: that a true personalist stance will clearly and inevitably require solidarity with anguish and weakness, a leave-taking from the advantages of privilege and position and a willing embrace of deprivation and suffering.

Although the personalist call was initially individual, Maurin envisioned as its ultimate goal a new, comprehensive structure for society, a structure that would not be imposed *upon* society by a revolution of force, but rather would grow up *within* society through a personal revolution of love ("building the new in the shell of the old," as the I.W.W. slogan had it). With Kropotkin and the distributists, Maurin believed that the form of that revolution would be voluntary collectives of men and women who would choose to reject the logic and the material rewards of the centralized, industralized, urban, consumer society in favor of a decentralized, craft- and agrarian-based, community-structured, creative social organism. Maurin recognized, with Marx, that a primary cause of dehumanization in the modern world—as well as a source of much of the exploitation, injustice and poverty suffered by the working class—was the loss of meaningful work, of significant decision-making power and of control of the means of production by the workers, those losses necessitated by the demands of mass production and maximum corporate profit. Therefore, like the distributists, Maurin flatly rejected the fundamental structures of modern, industrial society, viewing them as a kind of collective disease destructive of true happiness, goodness and spirituality.

The alternative Maurin proposed was a new synthesis of "cult, culture and cultivation" (that is, of *worship*, of *arts, crafts and intellectual activity* and of *manual labor* "on the land" to produce the basic necessities of life). The practical expression of this synthesis would be manageably sized communities of men and women living in self-sustaining, self-governing collectives, sharing in a balance of spiritual, intellectual and physical activity, expending their efforts to create things which were necessary, useful and beautiful, drawing their own food from the land, mutually nurturing and sustaining each other in a life of rich simplicity that was freed from the distractions of the useless, ugly, poisonous products with which a consumer society bought off the worker's desires for dignity, justice and meaningful labor. In such a society, Maurin believed, the distinctions between "religious" and "secular" activity would become meaningless and all of life would be a kind of liturgy, a work of worship in which men and women would participate in the ongoing creative and nurturing activity of God.

This corporate personalist vision—a social order in which there would be opportunity for men and women to relate to their work, their Creator and each other in dignity and wholeness—was Maurin's "green revolution" (as opposed to the "red" revolution of the communists, which accepted the inevitability of centralization, industrialization and class conflict). Scorned by many as a naive democratized medievalism which ignored the realities of human nature and the inexorability of technology, it remained the visionary goal of much Worker thought and practice well into the middle of the century. Then, Maurin's death, the merging of the laboring classes into the mainstream and the increasing nuclear threat all combined with the sometimes bizarre failures of various Worker experiments in agrarian communalism to push the dream of a new society incarnating the personalist vision on the land more and more to the fringes of Worker concern.

The last major source for the Worker philosophy—the tradition of nonviolence in the historic peace churches—would seem implicit in a truly personalist stance. It was clearly so to Dorothy Day, though when her pacifism came head-on with American enthusiasm for World War II and the moral ambiguities of that conflict, even many of the Workers themselves differed with her and left the movement to join the war against fascism. Dorothy Day held firm (even in the face of charges of dictatorship, purging of dissidents and hopeless naivete) and, 25 years later, it is the Worker conviction that war and preparations for war represent an ultimate kind of atheism, a final refusal to recognize the presence of Christ and the Kingdom in the world, that led Jeff Dietrich to the actions and consequent jail time that are the background for this book.

The specific history of how Dorothy Day—child of bourgeois gentility, active member of the Greenwich Village-Provincetown circle of the late teens that included Emma Goldman, Eugene O'Neill, Max Eastman and John Reed, atheist radical journalist for the *Masses* and Catholic convert—came, in 1933, in the depths of the Great Depression, to join forces with Peter Maurin—French peasant philosopher, nonstop talker, essayist and transient—to publish the first *Catholic Worker* newspaper (distributed largely among leftist workers at a Union Square May Day rally) is too rich to be detailed here. What is fundamental is that Dorothy Day spent the first 30 years of her life in a struggle between faith and commitment to God and a deeply personal identification with the suffering of the poor, especially working men and women. Until she met Maurin, she saw no way to bring together her two concerns. Her communist and radical friends had a deep passion for justice but no transcendent faith, no relationship to God. The church professed to hold the keys of the Kingdom, but seemed as oblivious to the suffering around it as it was to its own enculturation. Then, after an agonized prayer for guidance at the unfinished Shrine of the Immaculate Conception in Washington, D. C. (she was in the city as a journalist covering a hunger march), she found Peter Maurin at her tenement door. He proceeded to talk for hours, days on end, for four months, in fact. Out of that talk came a vision for what was to become the Catholic Worker movement, the answer to her prayer.

Maurin himself included three basic elements in his loose personalist program: roundtable discussions for clarification of personalist thought; houses of hospitality for communal living in voluntary poverty and service to the poor, especially the unemployed, and farm colonies (or "agronomic universities") for self-sufficient living, reaffirmation of the necessary connection between intellectual activity and manual labor and relocation of the broken inhabitants of inner-city slums. If publication of a newspaper is included under "clarification," then these three points became the basic structure upon which the various Worker communities hung their particular enactments of Worker philosophy.

Ironically, from the start much of the romanticism of Maurin's vision failed. In his free-for-all roundtables he apparently believed that if everyone talked long enough they would come to see the truth of the personalist vision. Instead, the first roundtables (in a rented hall) turned into shouting matches. Soon more controlled lecture-discussions had replaced them. Maurin also seemed convinced that the workers, the poor themselves, would respond to the message of personalism. Some did, but most "converts" to the Catholic Worker message were university-educated young people from the middle class, intellectuals (just as the leaders of the communist workers' revolution were intellectuals, not workers). Working men attending the meetings tended to be bored or convinced the movement couldn't be truly Catholic because no one had mentioned the Blessed Virgin Mary all evening.

Where the Worker was more successful was in the houses of hospitality that provided food and shelter, along with used clothing and a listening ear, to the unemployed and down-and-out of the inner city. The first official House, in the middle of Harlem, was closed after a few months because the landlord decided his storefront tenants—with their discussion groups and art classes for black children—were subversives. The first real House of Hospitality was Dorothy Day's own apartment and the adjacent rooms rented for preparation of the *Catholic Worker*. Peter Maurin brought home people who were hungry or in need of a place to stay, volunteers for the Worker moved in, eventually a soup line was established. The basic pattern for Worker Houses all over the country was set.

Primary to any Worker House (and most popular within the church) were the works of mercy. These works were offered in a context of voluntary poverty that left the Catholic Worker standing in real solidarity with the vulnerability and helplessness of the poor. Service—be it food, shelter, clothing or comfort—was offered from comrade to comrade, horizontally as it were, not from above by a comfortable beneficence. Less popular with many supporters was the Worker stand against those elements of bourgeois capitalist society that were seen to be the cause of the suffering of the poor (more than one donor instructed that contributions were "for the poor, not for propaganda"). Choosing the prophet's rather than the chaplain's role, the Worker remained resolutely within the church, but often as a moral thorn in its side. Rejecting the idolatrous myths of modern America (in fact, of the twentieth century as a whole)—nationalism, progress, consumption and a security based on force and violence—the Worker stood instead for decentralized worker ownership of the means of production and distribution, voluntary community based on consensus, the dignity of simple labor, active justice (as opposed to conventional charity), personal *metanoia* (repentance) expressed in acts of discontinuity with the prevailing order and a radically simplified life style. As the labor struggles of the '30s faded and the workers of America were more and more co-opted into the bourgeoisie, the primary focus of the movement gradually shifted to active nonviolence and resistance to war, a focus deepened by the creation of nuclear weapons and the permanent cold war with its prospects of global annihilation.

A significant personality within this shift was Ammon Hennacy, whose unique (one might say eccentric) approach to what he called his "one man revolution" touched the Catholic Worker for nearly two decades. Hennacy was by nature a loner, an egotist, a vigorous enthusiast for himself and his opposition to war, property and conventional piety. Although he became a convert to Catholicism (apparently mainly out of infatuation with Dorothy Day) and was, for a time, a faithful communicant, he eventually renounced the Church and through it all looked to the God he spelled with "a small 'g' and two 'os,' " a God which, more often than not, seemed a reflection of his own self-confidence. His particular gift to the Worker movement, aside from his being, indisputably, the most effective salesman the newspaper ever had, was his emphasis on nonviolent civil disobedience, public fasting and symbolic action as tactics of confronting the "powers"—most particularly the state— and his insistence that one must act, alone if necessary, even at the risk of appearing foolish or mad, but always act upon the truth. Where some, including Dorothy Day, saw zest and romantic fire, others saw braggadocio and insufferable self-centeredness, but—for better or worse—Ammon Hennacy was the third major force in the Worker movement and his particular style has special relevance for the approach of the present Los Angeles Catholic Worker Community.

That community, which has been in existance since 1970, was not the first expression of the Catholic Worker vision in the city. Five years or so after the Catholic Worker was founded in New York in 1933, a House of Hospitality was opened a few blocks south of the hard-core Skid Row district just east of downtown Los Angeles. Like its prototype, this House was primarily the result of the zeal of one remarkable woman: in this case, Dr. Julia T. Metcalf.

Dr. Julia (as her circle inevitably called her) was a spinster physician from Boston, a formidable woman (in her mid-fifties during the late Depression years) who wore a monocle and—in the words of one woman who remembers her—"knew how to tell off the clergy when necessary." Dismayed at the low level of intellectual life in the Los Angeles archdiocese, Dr. Julia and her sister in 1935 opened the St. Thomas More Library, the city's first and only Catholic lending library. It soon became a center for progressive Catholic thought, to which gravitated a circle of bright young university students, seminarians, teachers and religious. Regular Monday night "open forums" featured book reviews, discussions of contemporary Catholic thinkers and lectures by such visitors as G. K. Chesterton, (English distributist) Hilaire Belloc, Mother Margaret of Hungary (founder of the Sisters of Social Service) and Dorothy Day. The *Catholic Worker* was faithfully read and discussed by the Metcalf circle.

At some point in the late 1930s, George Putnam—a young convert then in his early 20s—opened the first House under the sponsorship of Dr. Metcalf and her group, but when he went east to seminary after about 10 months, the House was closed. Despite this setback, the Worker ideal continued to inflame Dr. Metcalf's circle. One of them recalls that they would go each May Day to distribute the *Catholic Worker* to the transient and unemployed in Pershing Square and then, exhausted from a day of radical fervor, would retire to the adjacent bar of the posh Biltmore Hotel for drinks.

On May 1, 1940, a second House—dedicated to Our Lady of Peace—was opened on East Twelfth Street, in the black ghetto just south of Skid Row. There are differing versions told of its founding. A member of the Metcalf circle recalls the group incorporating and installing an Alsatian ex-merchant marine, Jack Wagner, to run the House with his wife and young son. A contemporary newspaper column, however, states that Wagner started the House on his own, after working with Dorothy Day in New York, and that he operated it without official sponsors, a board or a regular source of funds.

Whatever its origins, the House was soon serving breakfast and supper to 150 men a day, as well as housing 23 as full-time guests. From the start, blacks were made particularly welcome (the only grounds for expulsion were drunkenness or racism). Clothing was distributed, rudimentary social work was done, there were lectures and films. There was even a Catholic Worker farm of sorts, after a printer down the street offered an empty tract of land in Yucca Valley to the Workers. Alcoholic men were regularly driven out to the fresh air and bracing simplicity of the high desert, even though the "ranch" boasted no buildings, not even an outhouse, only four tents that several times disappeared when guests left for the week.

In December of 1941 the war came. Like many other Catholic Worker enterprises throughout the country, the Los Angeles community was split between those who supported Dorothy Day's strict pacifism and those who felt the war to be morally justifiable, especially in the face of a fascist enemy and the "unprovoked" attack on Pearl Harbor. There were long hours of meeting and debate, much pounding on tables. Support for the House withered. Many young men from the Metcalf circle were going off to war. No one seems to remember exactly when or how the House was finally closed but before the war was over it no longer existed. The Wagners had disappeared, the printer had retired to his land in the desert, the Monday night forums had been abandoned due to gas rationing, the bright young circle that had surrounded Dr. Julia had been scattered by war, marriage and career. Dr. Metcalf herself continued to maintain the library until 1954, when she died after a long and painful fight against cancer. A friend remembers how few people attended her Requiem.

With the closing of Our Lady of Peace House, the Worker idea was dormant in Los Angeles for nearly 30 years. The war ended under the prophetic shadow of the atomic cloud, the "cold" war and its attendant lunacies were born, as were a "third" world, a civil rights movement, a counterculture, a "police action" in Korea and an apparently endless war in South East Asia. The Church endured its own internal convulsions as the Second Vatican Council shattered the conformity of centuries.

The present Catholic Worker Community in Los Angeles had its beginnings in the fall of 1969, among a household of former priests and nuns living in community in Pasadena. In that group were Chris and Dan Delany—she a former Immaculate Heart sister, now a teacher, and he a laicized priest, working with the American Friends Service Committee, who had known Ammon Hennacy before his death.

On Easter Sunday, 1970, the Delanys—using a van purchased with the "war taxes" they had refused to pay and carrying spaghetti cooked on their own kitchen stove—appeared in front of St. Vibiana's Cathedral (located next to the largest of the traditional downtown missions) to serve a free meal to anyone who wanted one. In contrast to the tactics of the missions, no sermon was preached, nothing was demanded. The site, along with its proximity to a major gathering place for Skid Row residents, had the unintended, yet added, advantage of making a visable witness before a chancery whose policies over the previous decades had emphasized suburban building programs over serving the needs of the poor.

After the first Sunday, the food line was moved to other locations within the area and in late September Jeff Dietrich—in his mid-twenties, recently returned from Europe, in relatively unthinking reaction to his traditional Catholic upbringing—joined the fledgling Worker community which, by then, numbered four and was in the process of renovating a former rooming house on Cummings Street in Boyle Heights to serve as a House of Hospitality. One of Dietrich's earliest memories of the Community is of distributing coffee, donuts and bus fare in the early morning to men being released from County Jail.

Early the next year the Cummings Street House was opened, named— interestingly enough—not after Day or Maurin, but in memory of aggressive rebel Ammon Hennacy. It was also dubbed the "Berrigan Resistance Center," with draft counselling and "sanctuary" offered for resisters, AWOLs and deserters. It was in January, 1971, as well, that the first issue of the Los Angeles Catholic Worker Community newspaper was published: *The Catholic Agitator* —so named, according to Delany in the lead article, after Peter Maurin, who "used to list his occupation as 'agitator.' " Compared to the sophistication of later editions (on the third issue, editor Dietrich changed the layout to one borrowed from *Rolling Stone* magazine—a far cry from the classic austerity of the *Catholic Worker*, which had copied the format of the *Daily Worker*), this first *Agitator* was high on passion and slight on subtlety or journalistic finesse and serves, today, as a kind of time-capsule of a unique era. There was a centerfold of a grinning Daniel Berrigan being taken to court (his manacled hands flashing a peace sign became the paper's logo), a primitive sun face was the background for a poetic editorial that announced that "What we are into is Life," and there were quotes from Whitman and Gibran, articles on Cesar Chavez, the draft and tax resistance. A biweekly "Celebration of Life" was announced (sounding like a combination folk Mass and love-in) and slogans like "END THE WAR AND FEED THE POOR, CLOSE ALL FACTORIES OF CRIME (JAILS AND PRISONS)" were prominently featured.

By the fall of 1971, the Health Department—after months of turning a benign blind eye to the activities of the street soup line—was forced to serve the Workers with complicated orders regarding their sidewalk operation and it was decided that a more permanent facility was necessary. In December of that year a site was found: an empty hotel cafe at 821 East Sixth Street, on the corner of Sixth and Gladys, across the street from the derelict All Nations Community Center and Settlement House, which was by now most noted for the number of homicides that occurred each winter in its cavernous, abandoned halls. Although the seedy transient hotel above the kitchen was still in use, the ground floor had been vacant for nearly a decade and had sustained heavy damage in an earthquake earlier that year. But it was large, well located (just outside the Skid Row core on East Fifth Street) and the rent was only $100 a month. On March 24, 1972, Hospitality Kitchen was opened, with a clothing distribution room operated from the rear.

While there was an apparently growing stability to the community's work and presence on the Row, its internal life was reaching a crisis point. There were differences of personality and style, with growing resentments over decision-making and allocation of funds. The end result was that, in late summer of the year, the Delanys departed, suddenly thrusting Dietrich into as much of a leadership role as the anarchistic, in many ways immature, community was willing to admit. Among other volunteers taken by surprise with this sudden change in leadership was Catherine Morris, a Sister of the Holy Child Jesus who had, until recently, been principal of her community's prestigious Mayfield School for Girls in Pasadena. She, like the other volunteers, had known nothing of the behind-the-scenes struggles within the Worker. All she knew was she had "been down on the Row helping Chris and

Dan and then all of the sudden they were gone and I was helping this little guy Dietrich." Within a year and a half, she and the "little guy" were married, despite a twelve year difference in their ages.

In February of 1973, the Los Angeles community became involved in its first widely publicized "action": the organization of a strike by Skid Row blood-bank donors. The "Blood Strike"—which eventually received national attention—sought to humanize and bring some small measure of justice to the trafficking in human blood that provided many Skid Row residents with their only income. Strikers' demands included increased payments, better medical screening, abolition of liability waivers, provision of nutritional supplements, "respectful treatment" and payments to a Union Health Fund," which would support a proposed medical and dental clinic for donors. A failure in terms of its designated goals, the strike nevertheless attracted the attention of legislators debating the dangers posed to mainstream recipients by blood from Skid Row sources. Strike organizers were called as witnesses before state hearings (which were eventually moved to Los Angeles) and the result was a state law restricting the sale of whole blood and the transformation of the banks into "plasma centers" operating under somewhat stricter guidelines than had been the case before the strike.

An ironic footnote to the strike was the fact that, on the night before it was to be inaugurated, a disturbed community member went on a rampage through Hennacy House, destroying furniture, throwing television sets through second-story windows and leaving gaping holes in the walls. By the time the strike began with Mass at the kitchen the following morning, Hennacy House was empty: some community members had fled downtown; one couple had simply packed their belongings and disappeared.

That frightening explosion of violence from within was a precursor to 20 difficult months that followed. Attempting to be obedient to Dorothy Day's council that the poor and forsaken must be received as equals in community and that no one who came should be turned away, the community opened itself to a seemingly endless series of disillusioning disasters. One Worker, brought home from the Row, stole the community car and pulled a gun on those who went after him to reclaim it, another turned out to be a heroin addict who cleaned out the house before he left, still another was discovered to be wanted for a $14,000 forgery in Texas.

By the summer of 1974, there were only three people in the community: Dietrich, Catherine Morris and David Lumian, a young humanist of Jewish background who had been president of his Orange County high school before joining the Worker. Among them, they ran the kitchen, the House of

Hospitality and the clothing room—as well as put out the paper 10 times a year. Later, in more prosperous times, Dietrich would recall many mornings when there was no food to prepare for the line of some 500 men that could be expected to form along Gladys Street and down the alley behind the kitchen. On those mornings they would pray—and somehow something would turn up, someone would appear at the door with a donation.

Toward the end of that year the Worker's fortunes began to change. Articles in local papers and a wider distribution of the *Agitator* were creating a solid base of support. New volunteers stayed on to become members, most of them young, but nevertheless men and women with serious commitments to justice and service (their tendency to long hair and ragged clothes soon earned the Worker the sobriquet "the hippie kitchen" among the men of the Row). Even the archdiocese began to take notice of—and a certain pride in—the only Skid Row "mission" with a "no ticket, no sermon, no limit" policy. The Cardinal offered his Christmas Eve Mass at the kitchen for the men and women of the streets and decaying tenement hotels. An "extended community" of, mainly, middle-class suburban friends of the Worker began to take shape, joining in the Wednesday evening Masses and potluck suppers at Hennacy House and attending the "clarification of thought" meetings on Friday nights. Students from Catholic high schools and universities became regular volunteers at the kitchen. The Worker was becoming dangerously respectable.

In June of 1975, a physician from the extended community joined with a Franciscan nun, several Hospitaller Brothers of St. John of God and the Workers to open Hospitality Free Clinic in what had until then been the clothing room behind the kitchen. From one night a week, the clinic hours grew to four sessions a week within a few months. The expansion of what was sometimes laughingly called the "Worker Empire" had begun.

In 1976, David Lumian moved into an empty room in the hotel above the kitchen, fulfilling the Delanys' original vision of Workers making their home on the Row, maintaining a presence among those the community served. Soon others joined him and eventually the entire upstairs was occupied by community members and their guests. Zedakah House—its name taken from a Hebrew word embodying the concepts of righteousness and justice—was born. At the end of that year, confrontations between Catholic Workers and Produce Market management over scavenging for edible discards from market dumpsters led first to arrests and then to a stall in the market, where community members joined with brothers from Mother Teresa's Missionaries of Charity to make daily collection and distribution of surplus, unsalable food. An influx of Latino immigrants into the previously single-resident hotels surrounding the kitchen led to the founding, in January of 1978, of *Nuestra Tienda*—an at-cost, membershp food store for Skid Row families.

In July of that same year, the community moved to a larger house on Brittania Street, a block from the first Ammon Hennacy House. The "new Hennacy" was a towering three-story Victorian building that dominated the neighborhood from its hilltop and included three other residences on the grounds, one of which was put to use for several years as transitional housing for families from the Row. In the spring of 1979, Justice Bakery was begun by Tony Trafecanty—who, with his wife and five children, made up the first family unit to join the community—providing work with dignity at decent wages for previous "unemployables" from the Skid Row population. Each year community members (now numbering nearly 20, sometimes more) vowed "no more projects" and each year new needs seemed to call irresistibly for response. In the fall of 1979, a legal clinic was founded by Ray Correio, Blood Strike organizer, and a year later a junk yard behind the kitchen was converted into a playground for neighborhood children.

In the meantime, the Worker had managed to become a major landowner. The original Hennacy House had always belonged to the community, since the Delanys purchased it in 1970, but the kitchen and Zedakah House above it were rented. By 1977, the original $100 per month rent had risen to $425 for both floors when a new owner—who resolutely refused to provide necessary maintenance and repairs—suddenly quadrupled that figure. The resulting negotiations, legal action and dramatic plans for a forcible eviction in the full glare of television cameras climaxed in an eleventh hour offer to sell the building to the community for $64,000. A fund-raising campaign—which included, at the suggestion of Mother Teresa, tying a petition to the statue of St. Joseph (patron of the worker and, coincidentally, of property)—raised over $100,000 in 30 days from donors as far away as Alaska. The additional money was used to purchase a small two-story building and lot behind the kitchen which became the home of an expanded clinic. Then, in 1978, when the Trafecantys purchased the Brittania Street property on behalf of the community, the "voluntarily poor" Workers found themselves the owners of seven buildings.

During the years of expansion, resistance actions and political protest in the tradition of Ammon Hennacy had not been forgotten. Dietrich's first arrest came in a November, 1975, "Dig or Disarm" demonstration in which he attempted to dig a bomb shelter in the lawn of the Pasadena City Hall to call attention to the absurdity of government plans for herding civilians into abandoned mine shafts during a nuclear attack. Throughout the mid- to late

'70s, David Lumian kept the community active in opposition to the development of the B-1 Bomber and the neutron bomb, to oppression of blacks in South Africa and infant formula abuses in the Third World. Beginning in 1977, the Workers began various attempts at street theater, including a Christmas "parable" about Jimmy (Carter) Claus deciding between weapons and human needs and an elaborate "Travelling Neutron Minstrel Players Review" that satirically saluted the neutron bomb as "a clean weapon that protects valuable buildings and machines" and featured a chorus of singing-dancing skyscrapers. Not all Worker demonstrations were so lighthearted, however. A Good Friday presence at the Seal Beach weapons depository in 1979 tied the traditional Stations of the Cross to the agony of a world on the brink of nuclear self-destruction.

Providing, as it did, a marketplace for the most sophisticated (and expensive) ways imaginable of destroying human life on a mass scale, the Military Electronics Exposition at the Anaheim Convention Center (one of several international "arms bazaars") became a logical target for the Workers' deepening seriousness about the necessity for standing in witness against rapid and uncontrolled escalation toward nuclear war. The first acts of civil disobedience in 1978 were low key but determined, with Jeff Dietrich, Kent Hoffman and several others peacefully blocking entrances to the exhibition hall. The following year, while still on probation, they returned, along with a number of others, and it was this repeat offense that resulted in the jail time—from October 25 to December 22, 1979—that is the background to this work.

In the two years since the Anaheim actions (which succeeded in driving the Exposition to West Germany in 1980, where it received an equally unfavorable reaction from peace activists there), the Los Angeles Catholic Worker Community has become steadily more committed to nonviolent civil disobedience and legal protests against the arms race, focusing its attention on Rockwell International—one of the nation's foremost "defense" contractors— and the Winter Conference (WINCON) of military and weaponry contractors in Encino, California.

Every Catholic Worker House has its distinctive characteristics, its unique personality. As has been noted, from the beginning the aggressive, confrontative, impious style of Ammon Hennacy has made its mark on the Los Angeles community, although this may have as much to do with the individual psychology of the community's leadership as with any overt influence from Hennacy's life and writings. The community maintains an activist, work-oriented approach that consciously subordinates interpersonal relationships,

They're selling our future in Anaheim

This October 23, 24, & 25, an International Arms Bazaar will be held in Anaheim. Its purpose ..... to display and distribute throughout the world the latest in sophisticated military electronics technology.

Protest this frightening event Monday evening.

OCTOBER 22

Join us at Stoddard Park in Anaheim, (on 9th St., South of katella) at 7:30 p.m.

Warning

From October 23-25, 1979, Southern California will once again be host to an <u>Arms Bazaar</u> (Military Electronics Exposition '79), the international gathering of weapons dealers displaying their wares to a diverse group of arms consumers.

The City of Anaheim has for the second year in a row, welcomed these war systems manufacturers, making it possible for yet another leap in the annual sale of over $400 billion in weapons.

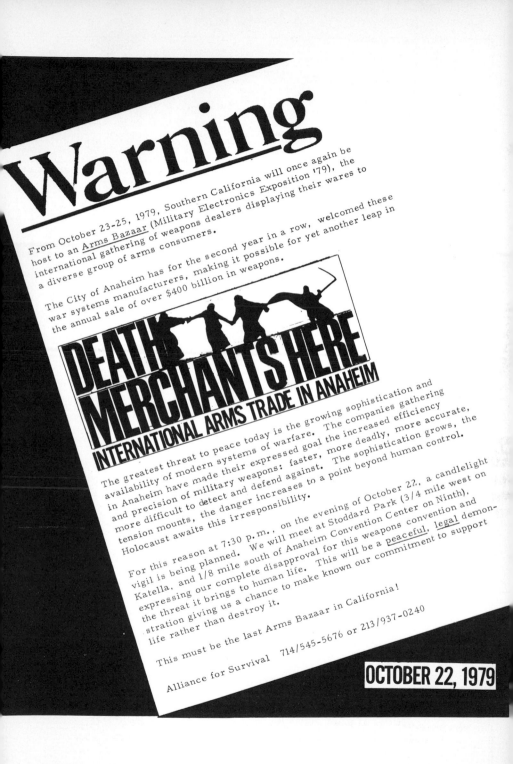

DEATH MERCHANTS HERE
INTERNATIONAL ARMS TRADE IN ANAHEIM

The greatest threat to peace today is the growing sophistication and availability of modern systems of warfare. The companies gathering in Anaheim have made their expressed goal the increased efficiency and precision of military weapons: faster, more deadly, more accurate, more difficult to detect and defend against. The sophistication grows, the tension mounts, the danger increases to a point beyond human control. Holocaust awaits this irresponsibility.

For this reason at 7:30 p.m., on the evening of October 22, a candlelight vigil is being planned. We will meet at Stoddard Park (3/4 mile west on Katella, and 1/8 mile south of Anaheim Convention Center on Ninth), expressing our complete disapproval for this weapons convention and the threat it brings to human life. This will be a <u>peaceful, legal</u> demonstration giving us a chance to make known our commitment to support life rather than destroy it.

This must be the last Arms Bazaar in California!

Alliance for Survival   714/545-5676 or 213/937-0240

OCTOBER 22, 1979

DEATH MERCHANTS HERE
INTERNATIONAL ARMS TRADE IN ANAHEIM

On October 23-25, international arms merchants will gather at the Anaheim Convention Center to sell and display their military weapons to any qualified nation with the cash to buy them. Expositions such as these are the cornerstone of the international arms trade.

Last year there were twenty-five such expositions throughout the country where military weapons were sold and displayed like vacuum cleaners. Buyers come from such sensitive areas of the world as the Middle East, Africa and Latin America.

Most people in Anaheim are concerned with the security of their homes and their nation. But the rising spread of military weapons, particularly in politically sensitive areas of the world can only mean insecurity for us.

WHY RISK THE SECURITY OF OUR NATION FOR THE PROFITS OF THE INTERNATIONAL ARMS TRADE?

1) Write to Mayor John Seymour telling him you are opposed to Anaheim hosting the Military Electronics Exposition '79. City of Anaheim, P.O. Box 3222, Anaheim, CA 92803.

2) Circulate the petition to your friends and neighbors.

3) Call Orange County Folks for a Future at 714/545-5676 or 213/972-9656.

Why Join This Protest?

U.S. and international dealers will display missile guidance systems, electronic warfare equipment, bomb and artillary targeting systems and more. This is not a government sponsored event. The public is not invited. This expo brings the horror of the Arms Race into our own backyards.

Billy Graham 1979

"Is it God's will that resources be used for massive armaments which could otherwise be used for alleviating human suffering and hunger? Of course Not! Our world has lost sight of true values and substituted for false gods and false values."

Activities Planned:

— Candle light walk from Stoddard Park to the Anaheim Convention Center, on Monday evening, October 22, at 7:30 p.m.
— Religious and political speakers.
— 3 day vigil from 8:30 a.m. to 6:00 p.m. on October 23, 24 & 25, at the Anaheim convention Center. Children's event on the 25th.

Please join us on any of these days.

For more information call:
(213) 738-1041
(714) 772-5089

We Need Your Help!

The Arms Dealers have millions of dollars, our only resouce is your support.

☐ Here's my contribution to help spread the word. $_____.
☐ Please send me more information.
(Please print)

Name_____ Address _____

City_____ State_____

Zip _____Phone_____
(Area Code)

Mail to: Alliance for Survival, 712 S. Grandview St., L.A., CA 90057

NORTH EXHIBITION HALL
SOUTH LOBBY
MEE '79
EXHIBITS · TECHNICAL SESSIONS · TUTORIAL COURSES

SURVIVAL

NEWSLETTER OF THE SOUTHERN CALIFORNIA ALLIANCE FOR SURVIVAL NOV.-DEC. 1979

Police prepare to arrest 68-year-old Betty Rottger and 11 others protesting the Military Electronics Exposition at the Anaheim Convention Center.

Protests Increase at Anaheim 'War Fair'; Exhibitors Decrease

"We can't be associated with this kind of thing," said one exhibitor at the Military Electronics Exposition in Anaheim after three days of protests shone an uncomfortably bright light on what the protestors termed a "war fair."

About 1500 persons—twice the number who protested the event last year—marched in a candlelight procession outside the annual arms convention at the Anaheim Convention Center on October 22.

Meanwhile, inside the exposition, the number of exhibitors was down 40% from last year's count, according to the *L.A. Times*, and a number of exhibitors said they would not return next year due to the protests.

The demonstrators were concerned that "increasingly sophisticated weaponry and technology are being made available on an indiscriminate level to countries throughout the world, and that threatens international security," said Kent Hoffman, a spokesman for another participating group, Catholic Worker.

A total of 36 persons were arrested during the three-day convention, mostly for peaceful blockades of the entrance to the exposition. Two of them—Kent Hoffman and Jeff Dietrich—received six-month sentences; they asked their supporters to write Judge Robert Fitzgerald in protest (for address, see p. 12). —*GB*

Radiation May Imperil Water in Southland

Radiation from the worst nuclear waste spill in U.S. history may be making its way toward the Colorado River, a major source of drinking water for Southern California, according to Dr. Joerg Winterer, a public health doctor in Gallup, New Mexico.

At least 95 million gallons of contaminated water and 1,100 tons of radioactive debris burst through a dam in Church Rock, N.M., on July 16 and flowed down the Puerco River forty miles into Arizona. The Puerco River flows into the Little Colorado River, which joins the Colorado River.

Radiation at the spill site went as high as 128,000 picocuries per liter, according to Jerry Klug of EPA's San Francisco office. The standard for safe drinking water is 16 picocuries per liter, says the Environmental Protection Agency.

The Puerco River is normally dry most of the year, but Dr. Winterer says that uranium mining operations are pumping water from the mines into the riverbed, thus assuring a continuous flow at least into Arizona, where the water often goes down into underground water sources.

Winter rains and flashfloods—as well as annual spring waterflows—are expected to wash much of the radioactive debris down into the Colorado River, from which water is pumped to 150 Southland cities by the Metropolitan Water District.

But Paul Singer, an MWD spokesman, says the waste—greatly diluted in transit—will be harmless. —*GB*

Newsletter of the Interfaith Hunger Coalition of So. Calif.

b ead

& justice

NOV. 19, 1979

Issue # 20

10

Anaheim police officers escort Marilyn Schafer, CSJ, after her arrest during the demonstration protesting the military electronics show. She carries a crumpled banner which reads: "Is This the Legacy We Will Leave Our Children?" Pope John Paul II. Details on page 5.   L A TIMES photo by Don Kelsen

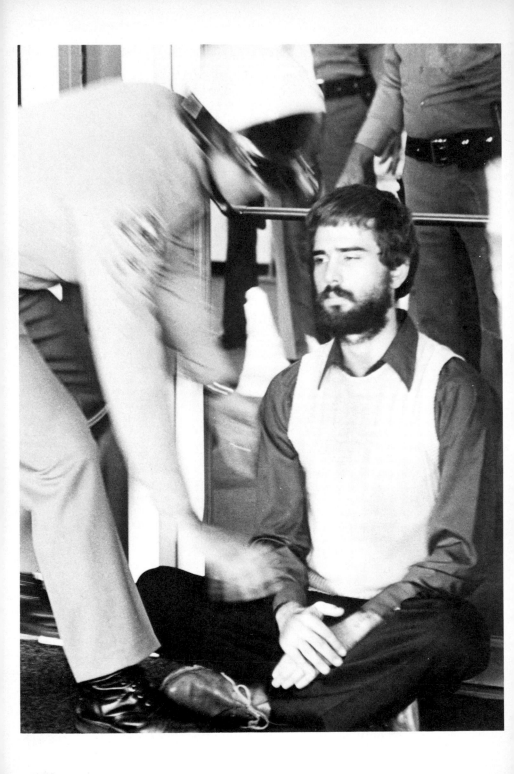

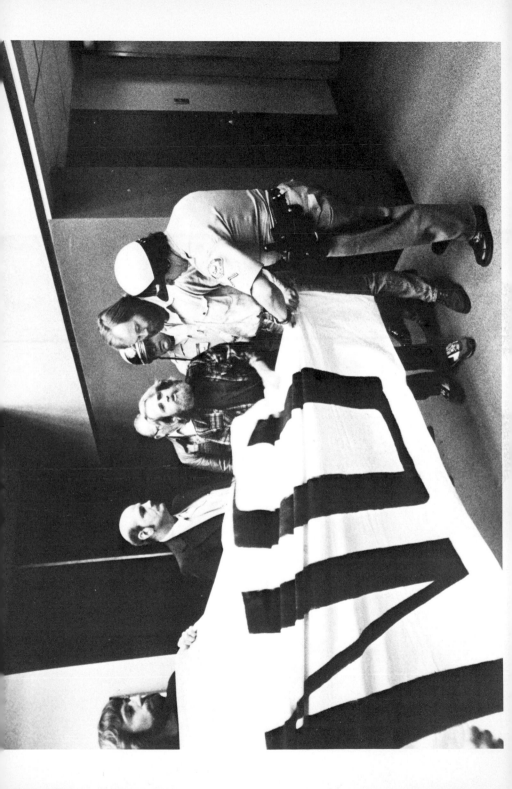

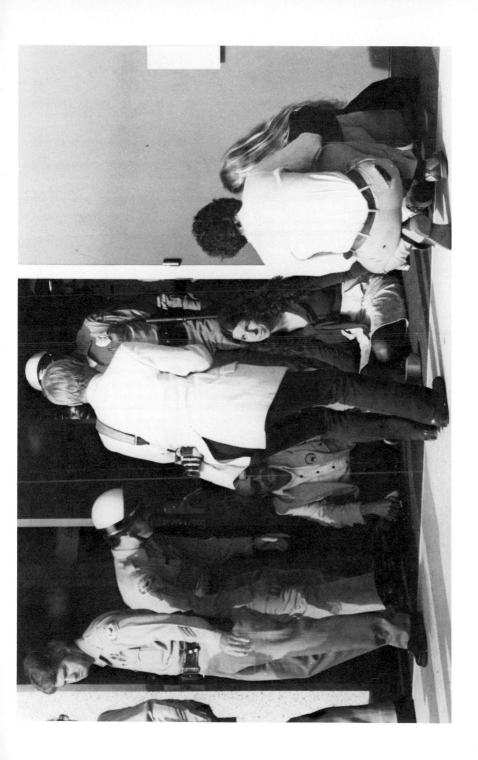

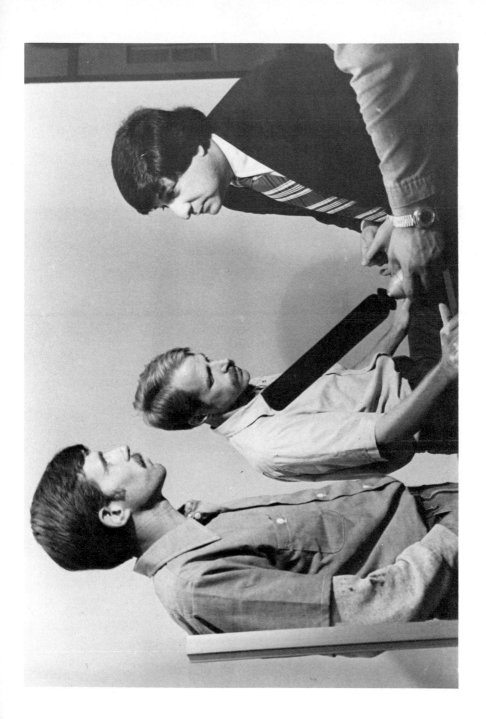

RELUCTANT RESISTER

The Prison Letters of Jeff Dietrich

Dear Catherine,

I just got back from the "Catholic services." I thought that it would be Mass. Boy, was I surprised when I finally got there and there were two men from St. Vincent de Paul who led us in saying the rosary! It was accompanied by a slide show on the Sorrowful Mysteries that would have bored sixth graders. Not too uplifting. I was looking forward to receiving communion.

My present situation is fine, but it is not permanent. Whenever I go out of my cell, I realize that there is a major portion of the population that I would find very difficult to deal with. I get a little frightened. I wish I would finally get into my permanent situation, so I can find out if I can handle it. I am doing a lot of praying. I never felt more totally in the hands of God. I miss you so much.

Dear Catherine,

This evening I washed the smell of fear from my undershirt, even as I tried to wash it from my own body. Furtively and quickly I washed, not out of modesty, but out of fear that someone would observe my small, spare frame. I feel like a tiny rabbit among so many hungry hounds.

The clanging of metal upon metal, my heart jumping each time— will I never have courage? The cold cement against my feet; the piercing draft working its way through thin blankets; the swaggering braggadocio of the inmates—life is indeed cold and hard and brutal. At this basic level, any act of kindness is an act of courage, a gift of gold, like water in the parched desert.

Today while I was working (I am a "runner," or errand boy, for Deputy Jones), Jones gave me a cup of coffee. I was profoundly grateful, not just for the coffee, but for the recognition of our shared humanity. So I waited until no one else was around and shared with him my apprehensions about new living conditions.

"Oh, you'll be O. K. in Tank D. Don't worry. If you were a young kid or if you were black, you might have some problems, but you'll be O. K. If you should have any problems, though, let me know on the sly. I know the deputies up there and I'll try to fix things for you without the other inmates finding out."

My apprehensions stem from the sudden realization that I am very obviously the smallest and weakest guy in a tank with 40 others.

Very little in my past experience has prepared me to deal with the raw, brutal, macho lifestyle of the jailhouse. "If they talk shit, just talk shit right back to them!" Can you imagine talking shit to guys with 20-inch biceps? That's how I measure the relative security of my environment—by the average size of the biceps and forearms. As I progress into the upper levels of the jailhouse social strata, I am convinced that there is a definite criminal morpho-type, and it's big and wide at the shoulders! Definitely not the Bill Rogers or Frank Shorter type that I strive to emulate.

I deliver food to the men in the hole and those in isolation cells.   I smile at them and try to say something to them like, "How's it goin'?" or "How are you?"   It sounds so inane, considering the starkness of the environment.   But no one has spurned the proffered kindness.

So far, the weight of the sentence has not borne down upon me.   I've been too busy being scared about each new change in the environment and whether or not I would survive.   I continue to survive one day, one hour, one minute at a time.   I pray unceasingly, I pray continuously.   Not the world peace or social justice.   I pray for survival.   I pray for mercy.   I pray for courage and strength, a touch of kindness, an inkling of compassion.   My life has never been so completely out of my control.   I have never been so completely in the hands of the Lord.   I am closer to the poor and powerless than I have ever been.   It is not a position I relish.   I would not choose it freely.   Clearly, I am insane, or under the influence of grace.   I pray ceaselessly: Lord stand beside me.

Dear Catherine,

"Do you have a degree or something?" asked Tim. "I mean you don't seem to fit in here. You look smarter than everyone else." Found out! Well, I try. God knows I try, but I can't get the swagger down. Somehow, it doesn't look right on me anyway. The shoulders are too narrow, arms too small, no tattoos. A Chinese dragon, anyone? Or a swastika, or perhaps the Virgin or a skull?

I try to make myself small, so I won't be seen, blend in with the environment. (No, just trying to melt into the wall.) But my job puts me right out where everyone can see me on the way to chow.

I can't talk in the low conspiratorial whispers, unintelligible grunts between clenched teeth, lips not moving so the guard won't notice. "Whatcha say, Ramon? 'S happenin', hombre?"

I am doing it all wrong. I smile when I hand out bedrolls: "Welcome to the County's free hotel."

"How about a little chef's salad?" I say when I help hand out food to those in isolation cells. "They just forgot to put in the ham and cheese, but the lettuce is guaranteed to be fresh, about two weeks ago."

I threw out the Merton book. Too pious and Catholic. It does not nourish me. I'm reading Berrigan. Some of it is O. K., but much of it is dated, very rhetorical, and full of grandiose hopes for youth and resistance and Simon and Garfunkle. Nothing to get your teeth into. But Niebuhr's *Beyond Tragedy*! That guy is deep, uncompromising, without illusion. The world will always crucify goodness. Every movement that takes power will ultimately oppress. Even the poor are not exempt.

If we ever have illusions that love and nonviolence will carry the day, then all we need to do is go to jail to have those illusions shattered. The world is based on power, coercion, force. It is hard to see this on the outside because we think that men's lives are directed by reason. But here, most pretensions of civilization are stripped away and the fist and the club rule. I do not believe we can change it. The human heart is corrupt and deceitful. Only by God's grace will the world be transformed. I continue to pray.

For years I have prayed for humility, a virtue which does not come easily to me.   But this process of stripping away leaves me with nothing.   The years of study, work, travel, aesthetic sensibility, organizational skills, leadership abilities, openness, enthusiasm, count for nothing here.   I can't even perform a simple task like serve food the right way, or make my bed properly, or keep from losing my towel.

I am without virtue, without ability, without any other resource but God.   Thus I pray: God give me strength.   God have mercy on me for I have sinned.

I think of you constantly, Catherine.   I know that my life is full of grace.   Otherwise, I would never have found you.   I would have moved through life without purpose or direction like so much flotsam and jetsam.

Dear Catherine,

Last night the big guys invited me to do some weightlifting with them! Can you believe it? Well, it's not exactly the way it sounds. The weight they were lifting was me! They lay under the bed at one end, while I sat on the top. They "pumped" the bed. Great fun, huh? Oh, well. I might not be a peer, but it's nice to be accepted on some level.

I feel a lot more at ease now that I am in a permanent situation and have a job and a routine. So far, it is a whole lot better than I thought it would be. Sometimes I even forget that I am in jail, and then I look up and see the bars and it seems so strange, startling, like being in a cage in the zoo.

All of our needs are cared for—food, clothing, shelter (perhaps more shelter than we want), books, games, medical and dental care. But the spirit can wither and die. I try to keep it alive by being enthusiastic and a little ironic. I greet people as I give them a bedroll, try to smile and encourage them. There is not much work to my job, so when I do it, I do it with a lot of enthusiasm and energy. The guards think I am an anomaly. They're not used to people who seem to enjoy their work.

I read the editorial about Kent and me in the *Times* today. I was excited and encouraged, very impressed that the *Times* would even notice our situation. However, I honestly feel that Judge Fitzgerald understands us better than the *Times*. The *Times* says that we are nice, responsible protestors and not a threat to society. But as Christians, activists, and agitators, we wish that we were a threat to society—against war and injustice and intolerance. Judge Fitzgerald has, in a sense, paid us the great compliment of taking us more seriously than even we take ourselves.

One thing I did note, however, is that once again it has been publicly stated that, as a person of "demonstrated conviction," I can't write a letter in 30 days promising not to return to the Convention Center. It's really amazing, I guess, that once you jump into something (or should I say fall?) like this, people just naturally assume that you are going to follow through and fulfill archetypal patterns. I am not sure I have the balls. I am much more modest than people give me credit for.

Speaking of archetypal roles, the situation in the courtroom was such a classic of high drama I almost wanted to say, "Cut! Cut! Now who in the hell is the casting director? And get me the writer. This scene has been done before." The judge was perfect as the pained functionary of the state who, though he finds that we are not criminals and even perceives our true innocence, must . nevertheless do his duty and protect the state from what is in actuality a threat. Perfect! And the two in jump-suits, handcuffed no less, behind bars even in the courtroom, degraded by every standard of our society, yet still erect and brave, ready to bear the brunt of injustice. Not arrogant, not bold, nor full of hubris, simply prepared to accept their fate. Perfect! And the tearful friends in the audience. Great drama! But the writer got carried away with the departure scene. Too much. Corny. Over-written. I mean really, it just won't play.

As they are putting the cuffs on us in preparation for getting on the bus, one of the guards comes to us and says, "Those were very moving statements that you made in the courtroom." Now who's gonna believe a line like that from some beer-bellied deputy sheriff? And as if that isn't enough, the same deputy says, "Do you think your friends are gonna try to block the bus?" There's everybody lined up outside singing and clapping. Now that really won't work! It's cornier than that last scene from *Billy Jack!*

I just got a letter from Joan in which she quotes the judge's statement that we are "celebrities." Honest to God, I never felt less like a celebrity or a hero. There is something about being here that is a real leveling process. I'm just another inmate and not a very outstanding one for that matter. I am completely without resources, fragile and ultimately dependent upon God. Please pray for me.

Dear Catherine,

My new-found confidence was short-lived.   Last night
"Mumbles," the guy in the bunk across from mine, told me some
horror stories.   Fights, suicides, gang bangs in the showers.   No
wonder I can't get any Vaseline for my chapped lips.   It confirmed
my initial impressions that violence is seething just under the
surface.   His advice, "Don't protest in here.   Just do your own
time."   Frankly, I hope the occasion never arrives in which I might
feel impelled to protest.   God, what a coward I am at heart!

Last night I dreamed that I had been released.

Just saw Kent.   His request to go to the minimum-security
facility was turned down.   The reply said, "You will do your time
here."   A little depressing and scary and very vindictive.   Clearly,
we are being punished!   I don't mind being treated like a "common
criminal," but to be treated worse than a common criminal, that's
tough.   It takes a toll.   People with records as long as my arm are
sent there, yet we are obliged to do our time inside the walls of
County Jail.   Not fair!

I got sent to the County Health Department today for a chest
x-ray.   Talk about feeling like a criminal!   First the handcuffs,
then the leg-irons.   Then along with two armed guards, we ambled
into the health clinic, while everyone inside and in the parking lot
averted their eyes.

More letters from people who think that I am strong and
dedicated.   If they only knew how scared I am.   People really want
to believe that it's possible to be brave, noble, pure.   I *hope* that it
is.

Dear Catherine,

Taking each day as a separate event is not so bad.   It only gets
bad when I think of all of the days all together; the weeks, the
months become oppresssive.   Four months—that was almost as
much time as I spent in Europe before I came to the Catholic
Worker.   That was such a long time.   So much happened, so much
changed in my life.   Four months—a lifetime!
Funny that before now writing has always been a chore to be
avoided.   But now there is nothing that gives me more
pleasure.   When there is nothing else to do and no one with whom
to share your thoughts and reflections, there isn't much
choice.   Also, the enforced discipline of the situation, which is
virtually monastic, almost requires that one become more focused
and introspective.
Each event that happens becomes more significant, bathed as it is
in the light of reflection and introspection.   The other day some
fellow inmate was riding down the escalator, singing "Day by Day,"
as it echoed and reverberated off the walls of the stairwell.   Even
though he couldn't sing at all, it seemed a profound, almost holy
experience.
Speaking of holy experiences, part of my job is serving lunch and
dinner to the "In-Cells," those in protective custody—sex offenders,
gays and snitches—the rejects of the rejected.   We also serve soup
and two slices of bread to the guys in the hole.   Today there were
seven of them.   I thought I would at least try to smile and be
cheerful while I served this meager fare, as I am the only human
contact they have.   But the door doesn't open.   A small rectangular
window below waist level is pulled down and the bread and soup are
set there.   A single hand reaches out and the food is gone.   No
hello, no thank you, no contact, no human warmth, no
communion.   Surely, man does not live by bread alone.   Never
have I been moved so passionately by the sight of a single hand.   All
I could do was silently pray, and the words "Give us this day our
daily bread, and forgive us our trespasses as we forgive others" took

35

on a new significance.   I had finally reached, within the secret recesses and labyrinths of this jail, the silent center and perfect still point of human suffering.   Behind those thick steel doors, entombed in concrete, curled in a tight fetal position on a cold metal bed, lies the suffering body of Christ.

Where, in God's name is *his* compassionate and faith-filled Church?   Where are the priests to minister to his wounded body?   Who will bring the sacraments to the wretched and rejected?   Who will roll back the stone and enter the tomb?   Who will bring the Good News of the Resurrection and Christ's eternal love to rekindle lost faith, lost hope?

Do not the cries of the suffering and rejected ones pierce the very concrete and steel?   Have you ears that do not hear, eyes that do not see?   Is your heart turned to stone?   Do you stand before us as the judges do—cynical, haughty, powerful—and deem us unworthy, unfit to be a part of his Church?

It's scandalous.   Half of the people in here must be Catholic, yet there is no priest, no Mass, no sacraments!   Woe to you who minister only to the rich and are unmindful of the poor, the sick, the prisoner.

Before I got sidetracked, I was going to tell you something of my daily routine.   I am awakened first at about 5:30 A.M. for breakfast, which I don't go to, so I roll over and go back to sleep until the call comes over the P. A. system for the work crew.   Get up, make my bed, brush my teeth, watch a little morning news on TV.   Get to work about 7:30.   Do a few stretching exercises until about 8:00, when Gilbert, my partner, goes downstairs to pick up the newspapers.   He delivers them to each of the tanks and drops off an *L. A. Times* and a *Register* for us.   About this time, the coffee is ready and the deputy lets us in the guard station to get the first of three or four cups of coffee for the day.

I then kick back for an hour or two and read the entire *L. A. Times*, while drinking my morning coffee.   Hard life!   A few inmates may come up from booking and we give them a bedroll.   Maybe we might sweep the hall or run a quick errand.   Nothing too strenuous, which gives much quiet time for reading and writing.   We even have our own room with makeshift table and chairs and, relatively speaking, a certain amount of privacy.

The next big event of the day is serving lunch at about 11:00
A.M.   One of us goes up to the kitchen in a big service elevator,
accompanied by a deputy.   We bring down a large bakery cabinet
full of trays of food which we serve, again accompanied by a deputy,
to the people in protective custody and the hole.   Usually, after
serving we can take a few minutes to eat anything that we
want.   Gilbert attacks it with gusto, as much for the extra privilege
to brag about back in the cell as the food itself.   Another privilege is
knowing ahead of time what is for chow.   There is a certain prestige
in having such info.   I usually refrain from eating extra chow, but
last night they had sugar cookies and milk.   Boy, did I scarf
them!   I even contemplated stuffing a few of them in my
pocket.   Fortunately, I didn't, because as we were pushing the cart
down the hall the deputy said, "I guess, as good trustees, you didn't
slip any of those cookies in your pocket, so I don't have to search
you."   The variety of life situations is so limited that they know in
advance what the response will be.

Next we get to accompany all the recently booked inmates up to
"late chow" about noon.   Gilbert does this; I don't eat lunch
either.   When Gilbert brings the new inmates back, we hand out
bedrolls and direct them to the door of a Box C tank.   I try to smile,
be encouraging, hand out a cigarette.   Everyone is really bummed
when they get up here.   Gilbert, on the other hand, takes a more
traditonal approach to the job, being somewhat more officious than I
am.

A few more errands, sweep the floor, a few more bedrolls, more
coffee, more reading or writing.   Then it's dinner time which is the
same routine as lunch.

Directly after dinner, at 3:30 P.M., we go back to the
cell.   Actually it's a dorm with about 60 guys in it.   I watch the
3:30 movie (lately it's been "Roots"; pretty good). The 4:00 P.M.
chow time only takes 15 minutes, then back to the movie until 5:00
P.M., read and write until lights out at 9:00 P.M., exercise for about an
hour, take a long shower, shave, watch TV or read, check out the
11:00 news.   Retire, read maybe, pray, sleep about
midnight.   Actually, I pray all day, but try to set aside a special time
also.

November 8

Dear Catherine,

Today is a milestone.   It's been two weeks since I came in here.   God, it seems like two months!   (I am stuck in this near void condemned to eternal television—cruel and unusual punishment indeed.   No day or night, no rain or sun, only monochromatic lifeless walls.)   They say that the first month is the toughest.   It does seem to be true that things have really improved since I arrived here.

Two weeks and my survival skills certainly seem to have improved, perhaps a little too much.   Yesterday, after visiting hours, they herded all of us, about 40, into that small cell, as usual, before having us ride single file back up the escalator.   Standing at the door of the cell was John, a guy I knew from the first tank that I was in.   My first reaction was to go up and say hello, but on second thought, I crouched down in the far corner.

John is the suspect in the sensational Orange County rapist case which has received extensive coverage in the Orange County papers.   His picture was on the front page of the *Register*.   After extensive talks with him, I am convinced he is innocent.

However, rape is not an acceptable crime in jailhouse society and I did not think it would do me any good to be associated with him.   John went out at the head of the line, I went out last.   I heard later tht he was "jumped" while on the escalator and punched a couple of times.

I am not sure of the ethics of such situations, but I am sure that my behavior doesn't qualify me for any hero buttons!

O God, I pray, give me strength.   I want to be strong, but I know I am a coward.   Please don't put me in situations that will break me.   Don't make my cross too hard to bear.   Help me to come out of this with the ability to do it again.   So much depends on it.

This morning one of the guys in our cell was called out: "Deputy Jones on the line.   Roll it up for release."   Those words sounded so good to me.   Even though it wasn't me getting released, I had an intense feeling of joy as I imagined him walking out into the predawn darkness, with the rain falling all around and everything smelling fresh and alive and clean.   I remembered that I had my running shoes here and that I would be wearing them and I would just take off running in the rain all the way to Bernice Ranford's house in Garden Grove, if it had been me.   But that's a long way off.

A lot of people in here, in fact, an amazing number of people want to talk about God.   Word gets around and they hear I am some kind of Christian or spiritual person or something.   I end up doing a little counseling, for which I never feel very adequate and talking about God for which I feel extremely inadequate.   My faith seems too cerebral.   I can't talk in terms of accepting Jesus as my personal Savior, or having a personal relationship with the Lord through Christ, or walking with the Lord.   These are such personal emotional experiences and, while they don't appeal to me, they have a profound and immediate effect upon the lives of so many people in here who need to be loved, who need to have purpose, who need to turn around the life patterns that imprisoned them.   Obviously, if they are in here, it hasn't worked yet, and a lot of it is just talk, rhetoric.   But some of these guys are really tough, and now they talk about the love of Jesus instead of who they're gonna cut up.   If that isn't *metanoia*, it is at least a very profound change.

Anyway, I am not thinking of converting, but my faith, my concept of Christianity doesn't have the kind of appeal that will change lives in here.   I have a renewed sense of respect for those evangelicals who preach the Gospel in prison.   It does make a difference.

Catherine, I miss you so much.   I love you.   This would be so much harder to do if you weren't there, so strong and vital.   If it weren't for you, I'd probably be selling real estate.   Come to think of it, maybe . . . no, just kidding.

Joan suggested that I should write a book about my life at the L. A. C. W.   If I did, I would call it *Reluctant Resister!*   O. K., guys, I've had enough of this game.   I am ready to come home now.   Too much reality all in one dose isn't healthy.

Wow!   It's hard to believe, but it's still Thursday, November 8, 1979.

Dear Catherine,

Whenever I start to feel relaxed in my environment, I am quickly reminded of where I am.   This morning when we came down to relieve the night shift, one of the guys, a very, very large guy, said something about "buns."   "What?" I said.   "You know. Buttocks.   Don't you fuck around?"   "No, uh, no I don't," I said, sitting down as quickly as I could.

I'm pretty sure that he was just kidding.   Well, not kidding so much as deliberately trying to make me feel uncomfortable.   He succeeded!   Anyway, he is not in my dorm and I rarely see him, but it made me feel like I'd really like to get out of here to Theo. Lacey, where it's less hard core.

The biggest guy in our dorm is a black man named Jesse.   We're pretty good pals because we're sort of "home boys."   He used to eat at Hospitality Kitchen!   When he was down on his luck, he used to get welfare and stay at the El Rey Hotel.   Small world.

"Poco a poco se va lejo."   I think it means, "Little by little we will get there."   I remember that it was on a little card in the office at Hennacy House for many years.   It continues to have much significance.

As the "Reluctant Resister," it has taken many years to get myself in real "trouble" because even though I know that it is the right thing intellectually, in my chicken heart of hearts I did not want to go to jail.   I suppose if there had been anyone around here even remotely like Berrigan or Jim Douglass, I would have been in this situation long ago.   This may come as a shock to some people, but I've never felt like a leadership-type person.   I am really much better at being a follower.   I have persistence, diligence, dedication, commitment.   I don't feel comfortable being an initiator.

I think my present situation is due in large part to Kent.   Each of us kind of ended up blaming the other for our present predicament.   "This is a fine mess you've gotten me into now, Ollie," as Stan Laurel would say.   Actually, I think, handcuffed together, we looked more like Mutt and Jeff.

Another factor that I keep coming back to is Judge Fitzgerald. I don't feel any anger towards him at all. At least, not any more anger or frustration than I would feel at anyone else in our society. We are all so isolated from the suffering and misery of the poor and war-torn. We are so caught up in the material distractions and pleasures of our culture that the prospect of nuclear devastation and its attendant horrors is a completely abstract concept.

Anyway, there seem to be some dynamics at play here that transcend the legal process and cause me to react in a way that I might not otherwise behave. Perhaps it's just a personality conflict. Perhaps it's more than that.

Last year Judge Fitzgerald's skepticism and his mocking manner which sought to identify us as neurotics with a martyr complex made me all the more determined to come back the next year. Now this year the same attitude combined with his efforts to punish us until we promise not to come back next year are making me feel as if I want to do it again, even though I had previously decided that I wouldn't do it in 1980.

We don't know what the dynamics are in this whole thing, but I do know that up to now, I've been taking tiny baby steps, testing my balance, testing the evenness of the ground, each small step only a slight calculated risk. Until now. Now it's suddenly a giant step that I really wasn't counting on. The ground is unfamiliar and my balance unsure. I don't feel the least bit in control of this game.

I keep asking God to protect me. How does it go? "Look not upon our sin, Lord, but upon the faith of your Church, and protect us from all anxiety and harm until you come again in Glory." I try to say "not my will, but your will be done, O Lord." But then, I keep thinking what if I don't like what the Lord's will has in store for me? What if it's too hard? What if I can't handle it? I try to have faith and believe that the Lord did not bring me to this place only to abandon me in my hour of greatest need. The temptation is great, but I cannot believe that my life is a cosmic joke. In fact, I cannot believe that life on this planet is a cosmic joke, which is what it would be if it were to end in nuclear holocaust.

Catherine, I love you and miss you all of the time.   I wish that you could come more often than twice a week.   Not to sound like a cry-baby because such behavior is not acceptable around here.   One must be real tough.   No whimpering!!!

Dear Catherine,

Since I heard that Joan is transcribing these notes, I have been experiencing something of a blockage.   I started to feel as though I should be writing something profound all of the time instead of these disconnected ramblings.   I started to feel self-conscious that I was constantly repeating myself and that I only had two or three themes, or that I was too concerned about myself, or too introspective. Well, I am serving notice right now that this is not the PRISON JOURNAL OF JEFF DIETRICH.

I need to write for personal, therapeutic reasons, because there is no one else with whom to share my thoughts.   So, whoever you are, you are welcome to read this, but if you are looking for something profound, you may have to wade through a lot of self-indulgent trivia to find it!

My folks came last night.   Boy, that's the hardest.   It takes a little more energy than most visits, because I want to make sure that I give a good impression, so they don't worry about me any more than they already do.

I am sure that this is difficult for them to take.   Having a son in jail is certainly not what parents envision for their children and is traditionally a source of grave embarrassment, particularly in circles in which my parents move.

Fortunately, it wasn't as bad as I thought it might be.   In fact, it was O. K.   My mother's eyes were a little watery, but I think that I convinced her not to cancel their vacation plans.

"There are plenty of people who are taking care of me.   There's not really anything that you can do.   I'll still be here when you get back."

"I know, but it seems frivolous to go on vacation when my son is in jail."

In a sense I guess that everything is frivolous in relation to the prospect of world annihilation.   But God knows I've yet to cancel a vacation or dinner invitation over the issue and, in a certain sense, my present situation is unintentional. Celebration and recreation are still a priority. Anyway, it would make me feel worse if my parents canceled their vacation plans. However, I was touched by my mother's concern and her feelings for the seriousness of my own situation have caused her to think more seriously about the issues that brought me here. It's not that my mother isn't concerned about world peace, it's just that generally we don't share the same perspective on how to achieve it.

My father has spent most of his adult life as an electronic engineer who has produced some of the very weapons systems that are being marketed at the Military Electronic Expo '79. He said that he was proud of me. That made me feel good, but I wonder if this whole thing will make any difference in his opinion about the need for military weapons. If it did, it might be worth being in jail just for that.

I know that coming here brings back painful memories of my brother's incarceration and death.

Sunday

November 11

Dear Catherine,

"As long as we remain sheep, we overcome. Even though we may be surrounded by a thousand wolves, we overcome, and are victorious. But as soon as we are wolves, we are beaten: for then we lose the support from the Shepherd who feeds not wolves, but only sheep." (St. John Chrysostom from Thomas Merton's *Conjectures of a Guilty Bystander*)

Yesterday, three or four guards were asking me if it was worth it to be in jail for so long. "It's not gonna make any difference, you know. No one cares."

There was no pragmatic answer that I could give them. "I honestly don't know if it will make any difference. But it seems important to do the right thing no matter what the consequences."

"You don't know? Hell! I'd sure make sure that I knew before I gave up six months of my life."

I thought about saying more, but how could I talk about something as ephemeral as God acting in our lives, or intervening in history. At such times, these sentiments ring too loudly of foolishness and absurdity. These men want to hear about results—mass demonstrations, political candidates, election returns, not the "foolishness of God that is wiser than the wisdom of men." How do I speak about the necessity of making personal sacrifice? Man is so hardened, so barbaric that only the spilling of blood, the sacrifice of human life can move him to change. Change does not come from the barrel of a gun or the decrees of the legislature. It comes out of suffering and sacrifice. And so it goes . . . the ancient ritual is played over and over again. Birth, death, resurrection. The light shown in the darkness and the darkness overcame it not. Only the sacrifices of the innocent victim will suffice.

In small measure, I am now participating in that ancient drama that is both immanent and transcendent, both in history and out of history, and finally makes history. I am completely conscious of the fact that I have taken on the archetypal role of "innocent victim." I am being punished, but I committed no crime.   In fact, I have done a service to mankind.   I am a prisoner, but I have no guilt.

It is a game that is both exciting and frightening.   It is the ultimate game, because at its more intense levels it doesn't allow for any "time-outs."   It's not often that people in our culture have the opportunity to immerse themselves totally in an experience, to become one with that experience.   In fact, our way of life is designed specifically to prevent us from having anything close to an authentic experience.

We are so afraid that we might experience suffering, misery, poverty, death that we have built buffers against these things that keep us from experiencing joy, happiness, satisfaction, transcendence, life and ultimately keep a lot of psychiatrists employed.

My father left $40 for me which brings my account up to $47.35.   I have trouble spending that much money on the outside.   If I don't smoke or buy candy, there's nothing else to buy here.   Oh well, I'll take you all out to dinner when I get out.

Catherine, I love you.

O God, stay with me.   Give me strength.   Protect me from
harm.   Keep me from despair and self-pity in the long months
ahead.   I would not be here if it were not for you.   I know that
there is ego and pride involved too.   But at its most basic, bedrock
level, I am here because I have tried to follow you.

On the front page of the *Santa Ana Register*, there is an article
about a computer foul-up that sent the jets off to Russia by
mistake.   They were called back this time.   But will we be so lucky
next time?   The article said this has happened several times
before.   The madmen are going to destroy this planet, probably
unintentionally.

I can't help but reflect that I am behind bars for trying to prevent
such an eventuality.   While they are still out there plotting the
demise of the human race.   Certainly is ironic.

Dear Catherine,

Last night I got the full details of the rape that took place in our cell just about 10 days before I got here.   They tied and gagged the kid.   Lots of people saw it take place but no one helped.   The moral climate around here is positively arctic.   Everyone is afraid of getting beat up, or having to go to protective custody.   Which frankly doesn't look that bad.   I just hate the idea of having to be protected.   I don't know how I'd act in that kind of situation and I'd rather not find out, which is why I'd really like to go to a minimum security situation.   I am just not ready to play with the big boys yet.   I get *too* scared.

If it weren't for these kinds of tensions and never being able to see the outside, it wouldn't be such a bad situation.   There is plenty of time for reading, writing and reflection, things I normally don't take much time for.   In a sense, the time is almost a luxury, a gift. Occasionally, people stop by my bunk and want to talk.   I find myself feeling impatient.   I want to get back to my book or my writing; then I have to remind myself that I've got plenty of time to do these things.

Mass is supposed to be tonight, but nobody I've talked to has heard about it.   Maybe it's like the movies that we're supposed to see on Fridays but never do.   I really would like to receive Communion.

What a great gift the Eucharist is.   There is something there which speaks so simply and clearly to my life.   Sometimes I think I am saved by poetry.   Without an understanding of poetry, how can we grasp the spirit of Christ's message?   Christ speaks to us through myth, metaphor, symbol, the language of poetry.

The Eucharist is such an excellent, perhaps even perfect metaphor.   It appeals to me intellectually, emotionally, physically, spiritually.   A simple meal of bread and wine.   It could have been bread and water, but that is prison fare, a subsistence meal.   Bread and wine, that is a celebration!   Bread for the body, wine for the spirit.   Body and blood.

How perfect that the first Eucharist was a Passover meal, itself a symbol of liberation from bondage and passage into the Promised Land, the Kingdom. The bread of oppression, the wine of liberation. The most moving religious experiences that I have ever had have been the Passover meals that we have celebrated at Hennacy House. Celebrations of political and spiritual liberation among friends and community. The extra wine deepens the emotional, cathartic experience.

Bread and wine, a celebration of life, death and resurrection, a vision of the Kingdom wherein all people may sit down to a simple meal as brothers and sisters and celebrate. The body of Christ is our nourishment, the blood of Christ is our liberation.

It's ironic that being locked in jail seems to release a whole flood of thoughts, words, reflections that, were I free, would never come to the surface. Ordinarily, I wouldn't have time to even think about some of these things, much less talk or write about them. Also, there is something about being here that gives me courage to express another side of myself. Perhaps it is that I believe others will know that they are more than just mere words. There is substance and sacrifice behind them.

It is at night that I miss you the most, Catherine. I know it is night when they turn out the lights. The bars cast a shadow pattern in the neon half-light. My bed is cold gray metal; sterile, empty, without love, without you. Though we are apart and I miss you terribly, I feel completely at one with you.

Dear Catherine,

Today is a very significant day. It may not be significant to anyone else, but it is to me. Today I had my first major bowel movement in three weeks. After I broke my eight-day fast I never really got back on a regular schedule due to a change of diet and lack of exercise. Boy, do I feel better! I feel as though my body has finally accepted the fact that I am in jail.

One of the guys who works in the kitchen is really incensed at my position as protester of military weapons. He is always on the verge of physically accosting me. "What are you, some kind of Communist?" "No, I am a pacifist and a Christian," I said. "Christian! If you are a Christian, what are you doing in jail? Oh, I know. You are a protester and society is against protesters, right?" "No, I am in jail, because I broke the law. I tried to block the entrance to a military arms convention." "What the hell do you think we're gonna do without arms? How are we gonna defend ourselves? If it weren't for arms, you'd be speaking Communist by now and working in some shoe factory!" "Well," I said, "I feel that if we don't do something about it, we will undoubtedly destroy the entire planet." "If that's the way it has to be, that's the way if has to be. If I can't have it, they can't have it."

That's it in a nutshell. We are totally possessed by fear and greed; our path is firmly fixed. I don't want to sound too pessimistic, but I believe that this man expresses the dominant opinion in the United States. Against such heartless sentiments, how do we prevail?

I find myself fascinated in a perverse way with American reaction to the Iranian situation. In no way do I condone the holding of the hostages. Though considering what the U.S. has done to Iran, it is understandable. It just seems a bit crudely done and indicates the lack of cohesion in the country.

What is most fascinating and frightening is the upsurge of patriotic, jingoistic demonstrations. Americans are witnessing the death throes of the empire and they are frightened and frustrated.   It will take a long time and we will make many people suffer before the final last gasp.   Perhaps we will even take the entire planet with us when we finally go.

I am certain that there must be a demagogue waiting in the wings to exploit this fear and frustration, who will charge us up "San Juan Hill" and into Tehran.   Surely this unscrupulous demagogue will make Carter and Kennedy look like ethical white knights.   We are definitely ready for a major revival of Americanism in all its glory.   Americans are tired of being pushed around, tired of being second rate.   If we can't have it, no one's gonna get it.

"As to courage, He will provide; and of course He will provide it more in the form of hope than as plain fortitude.   We must not expect to glance at ourselves and see 'courage,' and take comfort from this.   Christ alone, on the Cross and in the darkness, but already victorious, is our comfort."   (Thomas Merton)

Today I was thinking about what it would be like if I had to go to the hole.   It might not be so bad, I thought, if I could have a Bible.   It occurred to me that I had not seen any Bibles in the open cells.   Perhaps it is just lingering stereotypes from old prison movies.   Ammon Hennacy had a Bible in solitary, back in the days when it was still the practice to chain people to the wall, hand and foot, for most of the day.

Anyway, I asked one of the deputies if it were possible to get a Bible in the hole.   "No books allowed in the hole," he said.   "I know, but can you have a Bible?"   "No books allowed."   Well, the Bible is certainly a book.

It might be a good project for some church group or other Christian organization to try to get Bibles (Spanish and English) into the hole.   I don't know if anyone would be interested in reading them, but at least it's something to pass the time.   And I know I'd sure be glad to see it there.

Catherine, I am starting to feel self-conscious again.   I hope what I've been writing doesn't sound too pretentious or "profound."   I am really writing for you and of course for myself.   So when I start making comments on the demise of Western Civilization, make sure that whoever else reads this takes it with a grain of salt.   I love you.

Dear Catherine,

When I wake up in the morning I have a good feeling because it's
one more day down.   Each passing day is a victory.   (Tomorrow is
three weeks.)   Then I look forward to going to work and having a
cup of coffee.   And then the paper comes.   That's contact with the
outside so it is an upper to read it.   The next big event is serving
meals at 11:00.   I don't like going to the hole, but the rest of it is
something of a distraction and if we want, we can eat anything that
looks good.   Back to our store room.   More coffee, reading,
writing.   The store room is closed up for an hour and we are locked
in.   My partner takes a nap, a good quiet time for prayer and
meditation or exercise or reading and writing.   Next big event to
look forward to is serving dinner.   There usually are plenty of extra
desserts and milk to scarf down.   The sugar cookies and chocolate
cake are the best.   Did you know that Kent is a baker?   At 3:30 we
get off work and I look forward to dinner, but it comes too quickly at
4:00.   If it came at 6:00, the evening wouldn't be so long.

The evening is tough, because it's so long and there is lots of noise
and distraction—TV, smoking, loud card playing, slapping
dominoes.   It's hard to read or concentrate and sleeping is very
difficult.   It's a long unbroken period—no exciting things to look
forward to, except mail call, which is real important.   Keep those
cards and letters comin'. (Got a note last night from Dan Berrigan
expressing sympathy for me and "the other Catholic Worker
brother.")

The next big event is exercising, which is kind of boring.   I don't
look forward to it, but I take a long shower afterwards and that is
great.   A big step forward last night in my social standing—Tim
and Rocky invited me to lift weights with them.   This time they
really let me do it, not just sit on the bed that they were lifting!

Kent and the bakery crew came at 8:00 as they do every
morning.   I asked him what was for dessert.   Coconut cake.   Oh
boy!

O God, please stay with me.   I am so weak.   I cannot do this
alone.

Today, while I was serving lunch in the hole, one of the inmates
called out to the deputy that he was about to have a seizure.   The
deputy, much to my surprise, called on the phone for a nurse.   It
took almost a half hour for the nurse to come.   Good thing it wasn't
an emergency.   The deputy and I waited in silence.   Usually I
kind of banter or make light conversation, but not in the hole.

There were a lot of grilled cheese sandwiches on the food cart and
I wanted to eat some of them.   Somehow it seemed sacrilegious to
eat in this place.   Furthermore, the slight odor of vomit and the
fetid atmosphere of human suffering take the appetite away.   It was
not a good place to eat, but it was a good place to pray.   So I walked
up and down the cold, sterile corridors and prayed and felt very
strongly the presence of the Lord.

The hole is located on the fourth-floor mezzanine, between the
third and fourth floors.   We come down on the service elevators
with the food from the kitchen.   But most people come down a half-
flight of stairs from the fourth floor.   If you turn right, you enter
the hole.   If you turn left, you enter the chapel!   The chapel, like
everything else here, is sterile and lifeless.   The significant spiritual
experience that I had in the hole stands in sharp contrast to the vapid
religious ritual I attended in the chapel.   I couldn't help but reflect
upon this irony—that the house of God is located so near to the
house of punishment   I can say without a doubt that the Lord is
present ever so much more strongly in the latter than in the
former.   One is the true Church of the Catacomb; the other is just
simply buried.

Today I was told to go for a visit to the A-B building.   That
means Attorney-Bailbondsman.   It also means clergy.   I hate to go
for a visit there, because you have to wait in a little cage for up to two
hours until someone can come and search you after your visit.   I
hoped that the visit would be a good one.

Well, you can imagine my disappointment when it turned out to
be someone I didn't even know.   It was some Monsignor from the
Chancery Office with bushy eyebrows and flushed cheeks.   He had
been sent by the Bishop to see if I was all right.   The Bishop was in

Washington and would come to visit me next week. That's good. Now I don't have to write him a letter.

I am sure this good Monsignor felt he was doing his duty as well as an act of charity by visiting me. But as he did not know me from Adam and was obviously ill at ease, it was I who had to "visit" him. So I just did a running monologue about the jail, disarmament, Thomas Merton, prayer and spirituality, until we were able to politely disengage.

The Lord rewarded my compassion by not making me wait very long to be searched. I got back upstairs in time to help serve dinner and scarf down three pieces of coconut cake and three cartons of chocolate milk! Something I had been looking forward to all day.

In the *Register* today was another picture of a man that I recognized because I serve meals to him in protective custody. He is being tried in the sadistic murder and rape of a two-year-old girl. It was a horrible tragedy and people are all horrified by it, but we cannot seem to muster the same horror over the hundreds of thousands of children who suffer a slow sadistic death of starvation in Cambodia or the millions of others throughout the world.

Tomorrow is Thursday! A great joy. I will see Catherine.

Ernie (he's the barber) says I do my time easy. We'll see in a couple of months if I do easy time. But it is kind of interesting that for almost 10 years I have been striving and struggling to do the work of the Lord and now I do the most important work I have ever done, simply by doing nothing. So, in that sense, it certainly is easy time.

So far, everything goes well. I need to be more trusting, however. I continue to ask the Lord to protect me. You know— don't let me get beat up or stabbed or raped. Probably that's very juvenile, and indicates a low level of spiritual development. But what can you expect from a guy who ties petitions around statues of St. Joseph?* Probably on the existential level, it is more acceptable

---

* In 1977 Mother Teresa visited the Los Angeles Catholic Worker's Hospitality Free Kitchen on Skid Row. Members of the community shared with her their concern that they must raise $55,000 to buy the building within 30 days or be evicted. Mother Teresa counseled them to write down their petition and affix it to the statue of St. Joseph. Jeff Dietrich and Larry Holben, another member of the Catholic Worker community, went to the nearby St. Joseph Catholic Church and followed her instructions. Within two weeks, the community received enough donations to buy the building.

to pray for courage and fortitude.   For the virtues that are already within all of us.   Because while the Lord may see fit to subject us to any number of trials, he will give us the grace to prevail.   I hope I have that kind of faith anyway.

Recently my concern has been not so much that something would happen to me, but that I would witness something happening to someone else and be too frightened to respond.   As I prayed the other night, it occurred to me that I would have to respond with the same moral outrage to the violation of personhood in here as I would on the outside.   Whether the violation is committed by an individual or a government, it is the same.   I know that that seems elementary, but it occurred to me with such clarity that I felt as if I had more strength to do the actual deed, no matter what the consequences, and it gave me a sense of peace.

Dear Catherine,

At 2:30 today I was just reading away in my little store room. I
was all comfy and cozy. (Don't tell any of the other inmates that I
was comfy and cozy, O. K.?) I had all of the blankets stacked up in
such a way that I had sculpted an easy chair, with my feet elevated
just right, with support for my arms and back and a stack of blankets
next to me for my writing desk. Perfect. A fresh cup of coffee to
keep me alert. I was all set, looking forward to serving dinner in an
hour because we were having *cookies and milk!!* Scarf. Scarf.
Scarf.

One thing you learn around here is—don't get your heart set on
anything, because your time is not your own. Is this mortification
of desire? Perhaps it is detachment. I don't know, but I wasn't
too happy when my boss, Deputy Jones, called me over to the
"Guard Bubble" and gave me a pass for visiting in the A-B
building. "Oh, shit!" I said, knowing that I might be two hours in
the A-B cage waiting to get searched after my visit. "You want me
to find out who it is?" asked Jones. "Yeh!" I said, shocked at this
unexpected kindness. It was a priest who had come to bring me
Communion. Until I found out that he was bringing me
Communion, I wasn't going to go.

When I got down there, they put me in a small booth. What
happened next, I want you to understand, is an extremely charitable
rendition of the event. There is nothing like hardship to make one
more compassionate and nonjudgmental. But once again, as with so
many things that have happened to me lately, the stark irony of the
event dictates that I must repeat it. Even though Christian charity
and a sense of humility might cause me to keep it to myself. "Well,
get on with it," you must be saying by now, jumping up and down
unable to contain yourself. "Cut the crap and tell us what
happened, Dietrich."

Well, I was sitting in this little booth, not all that unlike a
confessional, except that there is glass on all four sides and the two
people can see each other. (I have to take a candy bar break.

Hold on.   I'll be back in about 10 minutes.   You need to get as
many good strokes as possible around here.   You know I am a very
sensuous and self-indulgent person.)

So I was sitting there in this glass confessional and in walked
Father.   I don't remember his name.   He was very short, about my
size and very, very round.   He was about 55 or 60, I would
say.   The sweet odor of his aftershave lotion immediately filled the
small compartment and reached me before we could even shake
hands.   He was, of course, dressed in black clerics, the front of his
shirt was stained, and he wore a gray narrow-brimmed hat with a
conservatively striped band around the crown that was strangely
disconcerting to me.

"You Dietrich?" he asked.   "Yes.   How are you, Father?" I said
as I stuck out my hand and grasped his in what can only be described
as a limp, tentative grasp.   "What parish you from?   What's your
pastor's name?"   Oh my God, I panicked.   This is a really real
Catholic priest.   I haven't met one of these in years.   You know,
when you run around with Newman chaplains, youth retreat
directors, ghetto pastors, antiwar priests, you forget that they still
make the standard variety of Catholic priest.   I didn't remember
what parish I belonged to, but since I go to daily Mass at St. Mary's,
I said, "I belong to St. Mary's parish, Father."   I wanted to say I
don't belong to a parish.   I belong to the Catholic Worker.   "Oh,
you go to St. Mary's in Fullerton?"   "No, in Los Angeles."   He
was disappointed.   Apparently he didn't know the pastor at St.
Mary's in L. A., so he didn't ask me who the pastor was.   Thank
God, because I don't know.

Well, that was the high point of our visit; it was down-hill from
there.   We sat on metal stools with a formica table between us.
Across the middle of the table was a glass partition about six inches
high.   One could reach over it if the occasion dictated.   However,
the glass was superfluous.   An opaque screen would have been more
appropriate as Father never looked me in the eye.   It was as if the
only way he could relate to me was in a confessional manner.

"Whatcher get in trouble with police for?"   He spoke with a kind
of Eastern European accent that made him sound a bit like a Jewish

mother.   He apparently knew nothing about the case.   "I was trying to block the entrance to the Convention Center where they were holding a military arms convention.   It was an effort to demonstrate our concern for disarmament."   Now he remembered that some nuns were arrested.   That somehow mitigated my circumstances, but not entirely.   "You don't wanta go fighting with police.   You get in trouble.   You come to jail.   It's boring.   You suffer a lot."   "But Father," I was extremely calm, almost amused at the total lack of comprehension, "didn't Christ call us to make sacrifices for our beliefs?"   "Well, it's a good cause, but you shouldn't go fighting in the streets.   Better you should go to school.   Get a degree, become a lawyer.   Then you can fight with words.   Then you have power."   "But Father, didn't Christ spend a good deal of his time fighting against lawyers?"

He ignored my question and went on with his interrogation. "You married?"   "Yes, Father."   "In the Church?"   "Yes, Father."   "That's good.   You got any kids?"   "No, Father." "Well, you should get a job and stay home and take care of your wife and kids."   He expounded on this theme for several minutes.   The first time I reminded him that I didn't have any kids, but after that, I just let it slide since he seemed determined to make me a father.   As all of this went on, he never looked at me.   I kept trying to move into his field of vision, but he held his hand up to the side of his face so that he could not see me.   Then he did what I had been dreading he would do from the beginning.   Oh God, I could of just died!   "O. K..   Now I bring you Communion.   But first, I hear your confession."   Gulp!   Yikes!   Oh, no!   Panic!   "Father, I went to confession before I came in here. (About 14 years before I came in here.)   I think I would just like to receive Communion, please."   (Oh, no.   Did I commit a sacrilege?   For a moment, all of those phantoms of juvenile guilt for sexual indiscretions loomed before me.   A sin of pride—refusing to confess.   All of this talk of humility and piety and you refuse to admit your sinfulness to this priest?)

Well, perhaps the Lord will be more merciful to me than I am and will give me more time to work out my feelings about the sacrament of penance.   In the meantime, I wasn't about to break a 14-year abstinence in this bizarre glass confessional.   However, the good Father did give me absolution, but I am certain that, though he didn't say it explicitly, it was "conditional absolution," and only takes effect sometime in the future when I do go to confession.

At no point in this entire encounter did I get angry or judgmental.   I was simply overwhelmed by the stark contrast of our mutual positions.   There was no way that he could relate to me or my actions.   We were both Christians, but both with a completely separate and distinct understanding of Scripture.

He had the same advice for me as I imagine that he does for anyone in this jail.   Don't fight; don't get in trouble; go to school; get a job; take care of your wife and kids and if you don't have any, *get some*.   This, then, is the Catholic chaplain of the jail—the man who is to bring Christ to the jailhouse population.   I have not seen him relate to the men in here, but I am sure that his charismatic powers do not get any better when he speaks to them.   He makes the two deacons who come with their faltering, awkward manner and insufferable slide shows and repetitious rosaries, look like rock stars.

There is so much that needs to be done, and so I should not criticize those few who are willing to give their talent and time, meager though it be.   I am grateful.   After all, there are scores of talented, enlightened Catholics in Orange County who know the needs and are more capable of meeting them and never set a foot in this jail.   Finally, this priest was kind enough to bring me the Eucharist, a Presence I am in much need of.   The Lord comes to us in strange ways.   We must always be open to that Presence in our life and try not to be too critical of the form it takes.

"God did not will that his people should merely live productive, quiet, joyous and expansive lives." (Merton)

Good news! Catherine said that we get out of jail January 17. That doesn't seem right; it seems like too little time. I figured that we would get out around February 26. Kent is going to put in a record check, just to make sure. I won't get my hopes up until I hear from him.

Bad news about getting into the minimum security facility. We have to write to the judge about it. I don't think that he is going to be too compassionate, especially when we are going to try to get him to eliminate our probation.

This is our third week in jail and I feel good. Truly a gift from God! I feel that if I come out of this whole thing in one piece (I still don't have absolute faith) that nothing will be able to stop me. I will have experienced about the worst they have to offer which so far isn't so bad. I keep thinking of the children of Israel whom King Nebuchadnezzar threw into the burning furnace. It was seven times hotter than the hottest furnace. And God's children who had refused to bow down to the golden idol were simply standing unharmed in the middle of the furnace. I think it's possible not just to survive but even to grow and flourish. A perfect revenge upon the system. This, however, is a provisional evaluation. I'll be able to give you a more definite answer when I get out of here.

In the meantime, I am grateful for the time to stop and take stock of my life, to read, write and reflect. I guess in a sense if it weren't for my latent anxieties, I would be very much at peace. Certainly I've never felt better about anything that I've ever done except maybe marry Catherine, but that's not quite the same.

I had a good surprise today. Because our cell was late in getting up to the roof (that's where we get outside), I was back from work in time to go.

The roof is obviously at the top of the jail. About 200 square feet of it is covered by a large metal cage, which is somewhat distracting but no one minds too much, because it's outside with real sunlight and real air and real color. There is a basketball court, a volleyball court, a ping-pong table and a handball court.   There are also eight telephones which may be used for local calls only.   No one plays volleyball.   The blacks and whites play basketball, but the real activity is centered on the handball courts where virtually all the players are Chicano.   I think they are born with a handball in their palms.   It is vigorous and violent and joyful.   It is a symbol of acceptance into the inner circle of the jailhouse elite.   Only the confirmed may play.   I imagine the same holds true for basketball at L. A. County Jail where the major population is black.

Well, as you can imagine, no one else was doing any running except for me.   Long-distance running is not one of the popular sports around here.   There I was running around the roof like some fool.   After I didn't stop for 30 or 40 minutes, people began to give me funny looks.   But it was good to run, to take my shirt off and feel the cool evening breeze on my body.   It was sensuous to breathe hard and feel my heart pounding and sweat stinging my eyes.   After a while I stopped just to look at the trees below, the blue sky and the bright reds of the dying day.

Honestly, it is not possible to appreciate life until we no longer have it.   We cannot have life until we give up our life.   I think so much about my life—the gift of community, my relationship with Catherine, meaningful work, the *Agitator*.   Never have things seemed so important to me.   When we are living from day to day we take things for granted.   Our bodies, our senses, the natural beauty of the world, love, warmth, community.   Now these are seen as from a tomb and they seem so special, precious.

Somehow from this vantage point, "precious" is the most appropriate word I can think of to describe my experience of life.   I see, as if I had new eyes.   I cannot take this life for granted.

Perhaps this is the meaning of Resurrection: that when we are deprived of life we come to appreciate it with a renewed understanding as one come back from the grave.

Speaking of Resurrection, tonight I once again made the mistake of going to Catholic services where we recited the joyful mysteries of the rosary.   It was anything but a resurrection experience!   I didn't make this mistake on purpose.   Kent wanted to meet me tonight at the "Catholic services." I said "ick" and told him what it was like. But on the chance that he might still go, I went to meet him. Apparently he took my advice because he wasn't there. I got there early and had to stand out in the hallway explaining that I was not being punished, I was going to the Catholic service (which may be thought of as a form of punishment as far as I am concerned). One of the guards said: "Catholic services are the worst ones in the jail." Though I've not been to any others, I am inclined to believe him.

The only words I can think of to describe the services are "insipid, vapid, fruitless, without meaning or content." They are not relevant. They do not touch lives. They do not address the experience of jail. It is an effort, but it is not a presence. The only saving grace of the evening was that the slide projector was broken and we did not have to watch the saccharine Sunday school "meditation." Thank God for small favors. Simply praying has value and meaning that transcends the obvious nervousness of the two deacons.

I appreciate the effort, but it will take more than prayers to touch the lives here, to assuage the suffering here, to be a living Christ-like presence. I am not angry at the feeble effort of these men. I am angry at the lack of effort on the part of the Church. There is such a need for a real ministry of service here—for visiting, counseling, family aid, a simple phone call.

Catherine, I love you. I am sorry our visit was so frustrating. I'll try to sort out my thoughts about what I want done so that I can be more clear. In the meantime, I appreciate everything you are doing and I miss you so much. I can't tell you again how much more I grow in love for you each day.

Dear Susan,

By now I guess that you know that I am in jail and that I received a six-month sentence for trying to block the entrance to the Military Weapons Convention in Anaheim.   I guess you know also that I love you very much and that I have tried to spend time with you so that you would better understand why I choose to live the life that I live.

I am doing all right.   Jail is not as bad as I thought it would be.   It is a little lonely and the time sometimes a little heavy.   But I am doing a lot of writing and reading and of course praying.   I feel that this is what God wants me to do and I am growing much stronger in my faith.

I ask you also to pray for me and to pray for peace and an end to the arms race.   As you can imagine, this is the most important issue in my life, otherwise I wouldn't be here for a minute.   I hope that you will begin to study this issue and perhaps even consider what actions you might take for peace at some point in the future.

When you come home for the holidays, please come and visit me.   Call Catherine and she will arrange it.   I would prefer if you could come without Mom and Dad.   I think it's easier for us to talk as adults without our parents around.   I also think that it is important for you to experience places like jails without the protection of your parents.   Jails are places of suffering and oppression.   They are the home of the poor and as such represent a harsh reality.   It is a reality I have tried to expose you to in your trips to Hennacy House.   Whether or not you respond to that reality is your decision.   I just don't want you to forget that it exists.

For most of your life you have lived, as I did too, in your parents' world.   It is a safe, comfortable, and very nice world.   Sometimes I wish I could still be in it.   But it ignores the fact that most of the rest of the world is suffering.   It is the call of these people, those who are dying of starvation and war, that keeps me from living a comfortable life.   The call of suffering people is the call of Christ himself.   I cannot keep my conscience quiet.   Pray for me.

Much love,

Jeff

Dear Bernice,

Before we were arrested, Debbie Garvey suggested to some of us that we try to do something especially nice before we go to jail so that when things got rough, we could close our eyes and think of it. She had spent a nice day at the beach before spending 10 days in jail last February. I decided to take a six-mile run around a lake. It was very nice, but I haven't thought too much about it since.

You know what I've thought about? Not a nature experience, or a spiritual experience, or a romantic experience. I hope this doesn't disillusion anyone who might think that I have much spiritual development, but what I've been thinking about over and over was eating steak at your house! Sitting in front of the TV, eating steak and drinking a six-pack. And of course your delightful hospitality. Boy, I guess that I am just an Archie Bunker at heart.

I am doing O. K., but please don't stop praying for me until I get out.

I love you,

Jeff

Friday
November 16

Dear Catherine,

Merton has been decrying modernism in the Church for the last 50 pages or so.   He is against a secularization of Christianity that would cast doubt upon such matters of faith as the Incarnation or the Redemption.   We are not to pat the unbeliever on the arm and say: "As a matter of fact, I don't find the Incarnation credible myself. Let's just say that Christ was a nice man who devoted himself to helping others."

But for me, as one who has come back to Christianity slowly and tentatively, it seems that just the opposite was true.   I had to begin with existence.   First, Christ existed as a man and the things that he did, the life that he lived, the values that he espoused and the manner in which he died are important whether or not we believe in the Incarnation, Virgin Birth or the Redemption.   Now it so happens that I do believe in these things, but I could not start with them as givens.   I am sure that I am misunderstanding this particular point of Merton's, because he rails at the kind of spiritualizing of Christ that destroys the significance of the Incarnation.   Anyway, it was important for me to begin simply with Christ as a man who gave his life completely for others, who brought people together as brothers and sisters around a common table to celebrate that giving.   This was a Spartan, stoic faith with a small *f*, stripped of divine pretensions.   In fact, I think I must have considered it a brave, courageous, even existential faith.   It was a faith in people's innate capacity to do good, faith in their ability to love others, and manifest the Kingdom of justice, in other words, faith in their ability to transform the world.

I am sure that this was a reaction against my childhood faith that came as a prepackaged gift from the Church, complete with all of the necessities for salvation—Incarnation, Resurrection, Redemption, and on and on, meaningless concepts—devoid of life, form, tangible reality.   Not the living God who comes to us in flesh and blood. My nascent, naive and faltering faith in a "demythologized" Christ

65

was inspired by my coming to the Catholic Worker. This seemed the place to begin building the Kingdom of love and justice.

It was my persistence at the Worker, however, that brought me to the realization that this was essentially an incomplete and inadequate faith. If we persist in trying to do good, trying to love others, trying to build the Kingdom, it eventually becomes all too apparent that the human heart and the human will are patently inadequate for such undertakings. For a brief period we can maintain the charade. But if we try to sustain it for any length of time, we realize that we are incapable of the selfless love and dedication and courage required. And so we turn to God. Or more accurately, we perceive in our moment of greatest weakness and frustration that we were completely dependent upon his grace and mercy all along. Our arrogance turns to humility. Then slowly the divine concepts begin to acquire meaning. We begin to believe there is a whole other dimension to reality than we had previously been willing to accept.

I hurt my back last night, so I have not been able to exercise today which means I had more time to write. Funny, I don't seem to have time to do all the things I want to do.

Dear Catherine,

About 9:00 P.M. I had settled down for the evening; the count had already been taken; the lights were out; I was munching a Baby Ruth bar and just getting into a trashy novel, when all of a sudden the lights went back on. People woke up bleary-eyed. What's going on? Over the loud speaker came a voice straight out of a Marine Corps nightmare: "Tank 21. Everyone in full jail issue. Take your shower shoes, towel, and all of your commissary and go into the dayroom and close the door behind you. You may have three photographs, six letters, and five books or magazines. The books must have your name and booking number or be issued by the Orange County Jail Library. If you have any extra shorts, socks, underwear or any of that shit, you might as well throw it in a pile in the middle of the room because we're going to find it." Surprise everybody! It's shakedown time.

"O. K. Everybody in the dayroom, listen up," barked out Deputy Smith. It is claimed by some that Smith is a long-time veteran of the Marine Corps and enjoys this type of thing, especially the strip-search part. "I want everyone in there to take off all of your clothes and step out here one man at a time . . . Hey you! Step out here, put everything on the floor. Hand me one item of clothing at a time. Run your fingers through your hair. Open your mouth, lift up your tongue. Lift up your balls. O. K. Now turn around, bend over, spread your cheeks and show me what you got. Lift up your feet. O. K. Stand there while I search your commissary. You only need five pencils. Right? Now take everything back to your bunk and get dressed."

I really didn't need to get dressed, as I had already been in bed before this whole scene took place. But I got dressed anyway, because somehow being naked I felt extremely vulnerable, less than human, like a piece of livestock herded from one pen to another, inspected, and certified. The simple act of putting my clothes back on restored a small measure of human dignity.   The lights are off now, but I don't feel quite like sleeping just yet.   Perhaps I will take a shower.

Dear Catherine,

"Prophetic religion is more rigorous than priestly religion.   It speaks an eternal 'No' to all human pretensions.   Priestly religion, on the other hand, appreciates what points to the eternal in all human values . . .   On the whole the religion of the priest is more dangerous than that of the prophet . . .   Many a church is more devoted to the characteristic ideals of its national life than to the Kingdom of God, in the light of which these ideals are seen in their pettiness and sinfulness.   For this reason the word of the prophet must always be heard . . .   But the unambiguous word of the prophet may do injustice to the ambiguity of the human enterprise.   That ambiguity may be the source of dishonesty and pretension.   But it is also the source of all genuine creativity in human history." (Reinhold Niebuhr)

Niebuhr is really incredible.   In just a few paragraphs he can outline one of the most basic conflicts of human existence.   The conflict between the priestly and the prophetic traditions is the conflict between the love of God and the love of culture.   It is a tragic conflict for which there is no possible resolution.   For Niebuhr (and I think he is correct in this perception), all human culture, art, music, literature, science, commerce, yes, even religion itself, is based upon the sword.   Ultimately these human creations are based upon oppression.   These beautiful human edifices rest squarely upon the shoulders of the poor.

It is such a horrible realization because we love this great beauty.   Niebuhr is so unrelenting in his perceptions of the human dilemma.   He sees that so much great art, culture and learning is funded through foundations like Ford and Rockefeller, and after all, where did this money come from except the poor?

Without the "sword" of government which subdues the warring passions of primitive tribes, we would not have the "pax Romana" of law and order, without which human culture as we know it would perish.   So Niebuhr will not allow us to fully espouse either the priestly or the prophetic traditions.   To be fully human, there must be a creative tension between the two.

I didn't really mean to start commenting on civilization and culture again.   I don't know too much about any of that so it would behoove me to stop making such far-ranging pronouncements. Actually I just wrote down the quote because it reminded me of my visit with the jail chaplain, which was a classic encounter of the priestly and the prophetic traditions.   But Niebuhr takes it far, far beyond my own facile perceptions of these two traditions.   He says that human existence requires both traditions and that neither one is justified in being fatuous or self-righteous about the other.

After all of that is said and done, I guess my visit yesterday with Bishop Johnson is somewhat anticlimactic.   Of course, when the deputy once again said I had a visitor in the A-B building, I was reluctant to go.   Then he checked on who it was.   "It's a Father Johnson."   Though he was about three days ahead of schedule, I was pretty certain that it was Bishop Johnson.

There really isn't that much to tell, honestly.   It was a pleasant and personable visit, though somewhat disappointing in that it was not more electrifying.   I was, of course, very flattered by the Bishop's visit and, as I have said before, not unaware of the archetypal significance of our mutually contrasting and complementary roles.   There was nothing of the conflict and complete lack of understanding that had been so apparent in my encounter with the chaplain.

Bishop Johnson is, first of all, a very warm and personable man.   The depth of his humanity transcends his pastoral role.   I was, I must say with all due modesty, eloquent.   Honestly, I have never in my life spoken so clearly or cogently.   It was as if I had been preparing for this meeting for years.   There is nothing like spending a few weeks in jail to make you more direct and focused.   I was almost embarrassed because I must have sounded like a theologian delivering a mild, but authoritative, lecture to the Bishop.   I spoke of Christ's call to peacemaking, the need for imperative moral action, the teaching duty of the Church.   I spoke of my own recent growth in faith and dependence upon the Lord.   I was, in fact, so wellspoken that I don't believe that I spoke at all.   I believe the words were inspired by the Holy Spirit, though admittedly I did not speak in tongues. That sounds a little pretentious, doesn't it? Well, all I know is that I can't take full credit for what I said.

The Bishop's response was something less than satisfying, but understandable. He feels that the leadership of the Church cannot get too far ahead of the people. Otherwise they lose contact and the people divide into factions and nothing can be done. The pulpit is not the proper forum for these "sensitive issues" because people are required to attend Mass. They are a captive audience and there is no opportunity for dialogue. He was not too open to a pastoral letter on the arms race, but he wants to establish a peace and justice center for the diocese.

Though the Bishop was warm, and human, and concerned, his main function is the maintenance of unity and cohesion as distinct from mine which is to proclaim the Kingdom. It has never been so apparent to me why I could never be a priest. Once, several years ago, my uncle, Father Brooks, accused me of wanting to destroy the Church. I have no desire to destroy the Church. I merely wish to see the Kingdom established. Sometimes the two are not compatible.

KEEP THOSE CARDS AND LETTERS COMING. THEY ARE SO IMPORTANT!

Catherine, it's so long until Sunday. I love you.

Tuesday
November 20

Dear Catherine,
    This is a disclaimer.   Most of this is quotes from Reinhold
Niebuhr's *Beyond Tragedy.*   It could get a little tedious but it is
very important to me.   It may be of no interest to the general
audience.
    Catherine, I live for Thursday and Sunday.
    "The contradictions of human existence which prevent power
from ever being good enough to belong to the Kingdom and which
equally prevent pure Love from being powerful enough to establish
itself in the world, must be finally overcome; but they can only be
overcome by divine action.   No human action, proceeding from
these contradictions is equal to it.   Here is the simple thesis of the
Lord's messianism." (Niebuhr)
    Apparently there were three concepts of the Messiah prevalent
during Christ's time: the political ruler, the Son of man who would
come from heaven and the suffering servant.   Christ rejected the
first concept while fasting 40 days in the desert.   He told Satan to
"get thee behind me."   His role as Messiah was conceived as a
combination of the latter two concepts.
    The suffering servant re-establishes God's eternal law of love in
the world, not by political or military force but by his very suffering
and powerlessness.   "The suffering servant does not impose
goodness upon the world by his power, rather he suffers, being
powerless, from the injustices of the powerful.   He suffers most
particularly from the sins of the righteous who do not understand
how full of unrighteousness is all human righteousness."   Into this
category we would put, I think, morally upright and good people like
judges, police, military, etc.
    "Thus when the Kingdom of God enters the world it is judged by
the world and found to be dangerous to all of its tentative harmonies
and relative justice.   But it also judges the world in the very
moment in which the world is condemning it . . .   The sinful world
is not destoyed by the Kingdom of God.   It is however fully
revealed.   Anyone who really understands the dimension of the

Kingdom of God ceases to have illusions about the world's kingdoms. He knows that their power and the relative justice of their balances of power are not the Kingdom of God."

Please believe me when I say that I speak in complete modesty and humility, but I feel very strongly that what happened at Anaheim and subsequently in court seems to be very close to what Niebuhr is talking about. And this indicates the "success" of our action as a sign and symbol of the Kingdom coming into the world. The very severity of our sentence indicates the success of our actions in revealing the injustice and corruption of the world's kingdoms. "The Kingdom of God enters the world in tragic terms. The 'prince of glory' dies on the Cross."

" . . . good men who do not understand the depth of human sinfulness, always imagine that sin will reduce itself to an absurdity and allow the strategy of the Kingdom a clear field. Unfortunately, there is nothing in human history to substantiate this hope.

"The Kingdom of God must still enter the world by way of the Crucifixion. [This next part is really great!] Goodness, armed with power, is corrupted; and pure love without power is destroyed. If it succeeds occasionally, as it does, it gives us vital and creative symbols of the fact that the Kingdom of God is a reality as well as a possibility. But if anyone trusts himself to it only as an established reality he will be disappointed."

It would seem that there is no escape from this historic paradox. However, Christ regarded himself not only as the suffering servant but also as the "Son of man." The Son of man will come in glory to establish his Kingdom. " . . . this final consummation will involve a transmutation of the whole world order. This new world order would not be some 'eternal life' of Greek conception but a transmuted temporal order."

The rest of the chapter gets a little too metaphysical for me. Perhaps I feel a little estranged from it because ultimately the Kingdom comes into being through God. Our feeble efforts are merely signs of the Kingdom that is to come.

"The will of God prevails when the Son of God is crucified. In that very crucifixion God has absorbed the contradictions of historic existence into Himself. Thus Christianity transmutes the tragedy of history into something which is not tragedy."

I hope this isn't too tedious or academic.   It is really important to me and part of the reason that I am writing all of this down is because I think Niebuhr sheds an extraordinary amount of light upon the contradictions implicit in the human condition.   I feel that I am caught in the paradox and it's important to understand it as well as I can.   If you don't like this part, skip it.

I've had some really interesting experiences (or should I say I continue to have some interesting experiences?) with the guards. Apparently, I don't look like I belong in here.   I guess it really shows.   Not much I can do about that except maybe more pushups or have the guy in the next bunk put a tattoo on my arm.

The other day I went to the kitchen with a guard I hadn't worked with before.   He kinda looked me up and down and said: "I hope you won't be insulted but you don't look like you belong in here."   "How can you tell that?" I asked.   "Just by the way you look.   I can just tell."   Well, we got down to the basics pretty fast once he found out what I was in here for.   He thought my position as a nonviolent resister was pretty crazy.   If we give up a single bomb or missile, the Soviets are going to invade us.   As soon as the hostages in Iran are either released or executed, we send in the Marines and take over the oil fields, solving two problems with one blow: revenge and the oil crisis.   As we were going back to the kitchen he called out to Deputy Lunger: "Hey, this guy is totally insane!   He doesn't believe in any military weapons."

After I got back to my store room, Deputy Lunger came in and closed the door behind him.   He began to interrogate me: Did I go to college?   What college?   Did I graduate?   What was my major?   What are my career objectives?   He then felt compelled to try to convince me of the absurdity of my position.   He was in fact a bit more intelligent and less jingoistic than most of the deputies. He thought that we should only use economic sanctions against Iran.   He didn't think there would be a nuclear war because each side had too much to lose.   He did not think that some smaller country or terrorist group would destroy a major population center causing an international outcry against nuclear weapons, which I think is a real possibility.   We must have talked about 30 minutes.   It was interesting and he was open to my perspectives, at least to the point of listening to me.   But ultimately he is a pragmatist and my positions are unrealistic.

After he left I asked Chips, my partner, who is a "home-boy," what should we do about Iran?   "I think we should give the God-damn Shah to them and get our people back."   It's interesting that Chips doesn't seem to suffer from the same militaristic, pro-American feelings that most of the deputies seem to have.

I don't think that I'll ever be a contemplative.   I've tried to set aside a time for prayer and meditation but I just can't seem to get into it.   I think, like most people, I only pray when I am frightened, which gives me ample opportunity for prayer around here.

I feel the most secure when I am at work.   It is comfortable, very few people around, the deputies know me, at least in the sense that I am not just a booking number.   It's quiet; it feels the least like jail to me.   The next best place is the mod (cell).   The other guys are O. K.   It's a little loud and raucous but not threatening.   I pray as I go to sleep at night.

I pray at times when the void seems to open up before me and suddenly I am totally alone with my fears.   I pray when I serve chow in the hole.   I pray when I am locked in small cages for hours with a group of other men.   I pray when I march in single file through the chow line and I can sense the undertone of violence and terror and desperation crackling through the air like static electricity.   I pray when I ride down the escalators and walk through the mausoleum halls alone and the cold cement and steel begin to wrap themselves around my heart.   I pray when the guards put their hands upon my body so that I feel like an animal or a piece of dirty laundry.   Only prayer can make sense out of this experience, only prayer can transform this experience.

Dear Catherine,

Last night was a bit loud in the mod.   But I went to sleep to the
sounds of a couple of home-boys singing old rock and roll tunes such
as "In the Still of the Night."

Just saw Kent.   He met with a lawyer last night who told him
that the probation that Fitzgerald put us on is ineffectual because we
are now serving the maximum sentence and Fitzgerald couldn't
violate us.   The lawyer knows him, and apparently Fitzgerald thinks
that we are terrorists!   Nonviolent terrorists, but still terrorists
nonetheless.   I knew that guy overrated us.   I have mixed reactions
to this new appellation.   I don't like being a terrorist, but on the
other hand a nonviolent terrorist is sort of glamorous.   It also
sounds as if you are determined and that you mean business.
Maybe next year we can nonviolently block the entrance to the
Convention Center *after* everyone is *inside* and hold the participants
hostage until the City of Anaheim agrees to turn over all weapons
manufacturers residing within their boundaries for trial.

When I got to work this morning the guy that I have mentioned
before suggested again jokingly that I should have oral sex with
him.   I said it was too early in the morning and that I hadn't had
my coffee yet.   He laughed at my wit.   I thought I was pretty
sharp for that early in the morning.   Especially considering my
abject terror!

Another deputy asked me about Iran just now.   "Are you the one
against sending troops into Iran?   What if it was your wife that they
had over there and they executed her?"   "My wife feels the same
way that I do."   "You should be on a boat to China."   "Why, they
are just as militaristic as the United States."   My reputation must
be spreading.   All of the deputies want to check it out and make
sure that there really is someone as crazy as they had heard I was.

I am getting a lot of messages from home over the TV.   The
other night I got up around 2:00 A.M. to relieve my kidneys.   I
could hear the TV on in the dayroom.   It was the news and I heard

something about Skid Row.   When I went in, who should be on the old tube but Larry Holben looking very saintly and Old Testament-like with his bushy beard, expounding on the needs of Skid Row children.   I got really homesick when I saw pictures of the Regal Hotel.   The announcer said Mr. Holben was a member of the Catholic Workers Committee.   There were a few die-hards still in the room watching this.   They didn't see me but I heard one of them say: "That's where that protester dude is from."

Last week I saw coverage of the gun battle at the Ellis Hotel.   Must have kept Zedakah House awake.*

When I went to work this morning I noticed that Sam wasn't among those who went down the escalator with us. "Hey, where's Sam?" "They called him out at 6:00 this morning. Took him to the pen today."

I was disappointed. I had hoped to say good-bye to Sam. I knew that he was going to the pen today but I thought I'd see him before he went. Sam wasn't exactly a great pal of mine but he tolerated and accepted me and I appreciated that as much as anything else that's happened to me recently.

Sam was a big, heavy-set Mexican "vato" about 35 years old, with enormous tattoos all over his body. He was in bunk 1 and he was sort of tacitly in charge. By force of his superior personality, you might say. The first night I was in the mod, I was taking a furtive shower after the lights went out, hoping that no one else would want to use the shower while I was in there. The shower curtain was suddenly pulled back in such a ferocious manner that I almost jumped out of my white, white skin. Only extreme self-control kept me from crying out. Standing there in his shorts, dark matted hair covering every inch of his thick, stocky, gorilla-like body, his abundant Pancho Villa style mustache appeared to curl in disgust at the sight of my naked white body. I had visions of that classic Humphrey Bogart bandito encounter in "Treasure of the Sierra Madre." "What's in the bags,

---

*Zedakah House is the name of the quarters above the Catholic Worker soup kitchen where several members of the community live and provide hospitality for homeless persons from Skid Row.

American?" Sam was so disgusted that he didn't even come in. I got out as quickly as I could.

I saw Sam several times in the course of my work each day. He would come into my store room for extra blankets and towels. He would speak very jovially to my partner, Chips, but completely ignore my existence. After a suitable length of time, however, Sam finally deigned to take enough notice of me to make me the butt of jokes and witticisms. "Looks like this newspaper was messed up by a demonstrator or something." The relationship was ultimately never what you would call warm. But it was tolerant, for which I was grateful, because it made me feel somewhat at "home," as if I might be able to make it here after all.

Just two days before they came and got Sam, I was taking my evening shower when Sam stepped in to use the shower next to me. I felt a little stupid because I was standing under the nozzle washing my undershirt and socks, and that just didn't seem very cool. But Sam took off his shorts and started to wash them, so I felt much cooler, like I was into the scene. I said hello to him. He said hello to me. Then there was just silence and running water. After a long while I finally got up my nerve and asked, "How long you in for, Sam?" "I'll probably be out of here Wednesday. They're taking me to the pen." "How come?" "For a burglary. And the shit of it is I don't even remember doin' it." "What do you mean?" "Oh, I ain't sayin' I haven't done anything cuz I done a lot of stuff but I always remember what I done." "So if you don't remember this one, you probably didn't do it, right?" "Right! But I got so many priors that I couldn't afford to fight it. And they had a witness who swears that she saw me there. It's not like I never done anything. I just don't remember doin' this one. So anyway I pleaded guilty and took the three years 'cause if I fought it and lost, the judge would'a given me nine years." "You been to the joint before?" I asked. "Oh yeh, three times before. It ain't so bad." "You married?" "No." "Well, maybe that's a thing," I said, feeling stupid for having said it, but not able to think of an appropriate response. I stood drying off trying not to look directly at Sam's hairy body, or the tattoo of a woman on his backside or his uncircumcised genitals. Awkward silence again prevailed as I tried desperately to think of some encouraging sentiment to exit by. Something sympathetic and yet still tough. "I'll pray for you, Sam," I said as I stepped out of the shower. That wasn't exactly what I had in mind. It just kind of came out while I wasn't thinking. It was the kind of thing that you would say at a funeral. It always sounds so false, hollow, inappropriate. Sam just kind of smiled like it was funny and wouldn't be much help where he was going, but it somehow was important to him anyway.

I've been praying for Sam ever since. Maybe I'll be praying for Sam for the rest of my life. Remember Sam in the prayers of the faithful.

Dear Catherine,

I got to go up to the roof area again today. Each time it looks more beautiful outside than it did the last time. Actually, though, objectively speaking, I think it was more beautiful today than it has been in quite a while. The desert winds had cleared the air of smog, the mountains were visible with a bit of snow on the slopes and a few clouds. I could see Palos Verdes and the ocean. Everything stood out brilliantly, bright, green and alive.

Three other guys joined me today at various times in my jog around the roof. Perhaps my social standing is improving.

Niebuhr is so harsh and uncompromising in his perception of the human soul. He does not allow us to have any pretensions about ourselves. It is not that difficult for the prophet to turn into a pharisee. Our vision of God's Kingdom is only a partial one. We are but the remnants of the Light. One day the total vision will be restored.

You may have to put up with Niebuhr for quite a while because I've decided to re-read his book *Beyond Tragedy*.

So the basic human condition is insecurity. Man is eternally subject to famine, pestilence, disease, war, death. His greatest desire is to live in security. The false prophet will offer this security. Among the false prophets are: the priest who offers the security of God's protection against life's vicissitudes to those who believe; the politician who offers the security of the nation/state's protection against war; the man of commerce who offers the security of a stable economy and the vision of a peaceful world subdued by the mutuality of world trade; the physician who, though he offers us protection against disease, cannot, as much as we might delude ourselves into thinking so, offer us protection against death.

The test of the true prophet is that he does not offer security because: "All societies and individuals therefore remain under the judgment and doom of God. Their hope must therefore always lie in a *mercy* which is able to overrule the angry passions of men, in a

Kingdom of God which will bring the kingdom of sin to naught."
(Niebuhr)

Niebuhr goes on to say that the prophet himself comes also under God's judgment: "Wherefore he must speak humbly." No one gets off the hook. We are all sinners and stand in equal need of God's mercy. Actually I should say that we are all guilty of human existence.

I hope you find this interesting. I know I keep harping on the theme of prophets but it is something very much on my mind of late, like the last three weeks. Also I didn't know the Niebuhr book was so concerned with this theme when I requested it. Perhaps it is providential. Well, I guess all things are providential. Anyway I hope this doesn't start sounding like a sophomoric term paper.

Last night I had a rather interesting dream. I usually don't remember my dreams, though I am a real fan of Carl Jung. The ones that I do remember are most often so dull that they don't bear repeating. They never have any of those great Jungian symbols like birds or water or fire or the wise old man, and further they are always in black and white. I must have an extremely dull unconscious mind.

After all of that introduction, I hope the dream will be worth it. There is not all that much to it, but it had some interesting symbols in it. First of all, it is in a church. I am sitting in church with my parents and there is a rock singer on the altar dressed in an outlandish costume. He looks something like a punk rock type. He's playing a guitar and singing and there is smoke around his feet and lower legs as if from some kind of fog machine. My father says, "What do you think of that guy?" I say that I think he is really weird and I never could accept something like that. "Well, why didn't you ever tell me that?" says my father. "I thought I had," and then we fall into each other's arms and start crying.

I don't think I'll interpret that. But I remember waking with a feeling of catharsis. Oh, well. So much for dreams. I don't dream about getting out of here, but I sure think about it a lot. I can't believe that it's not even been a month.

I'm looking forward to Thanksgiving. That will mark almost a month. Then Christmas will mark two months. I don't think it will hassle me too much to miss the holidays. We make too much of these celebrations so that they become trivialized, sentimentalized and soppy.

But celebration is one of the things that I do think about, especially when I think of getting out of here. One of my favorite fantasies is a big party with all of our friends. God, it will be an historic blast! In fact, I envision a rather long season of celebration what with Kent and me getting out of jail, a belated Christmas party, the ten-year L. A. C. W. anniversary, my birthday party (March 11), our sixth wedding anniversary. This time of celebration has special poignancy for me because I recently realized the intimate connection between celebration and suffering.

Dear Catherine,

The wind whistles
Down cream-white corridors
Of cement
As if through infinite canyons
Of desperation.

A skin-piercing chill
That grips the very heart.

Up endless escalators,
It whips through tiers and tiers
Of latticed, barred cells.

The prisoners,
Hands stuffed in pockets,
Heads bowed,
Like medieval monks
Shuffle in silence.

Along cream-colored corridors
Of cement they move
Through endless canyons
Of despair and desolation.

Battered and barred,
Caught and caged.

As the lights go out at night I am not so much lonely as just
alone.   I have never had quite this sense of self before, a feeling of
compression, distillation, essence.

The boys have taken to gathering in the bathroom after lights out
for exercise and bullshit.   The addition of a couple of new faces
made it a little more raucous and exceedingly more macho.

Dear Catherine,

Another milestone.　Four weeks are past.　By the way, four
weeks don't equal a month here.　Four weeks is 28 days.　It'll be
three more days before I am here a month.　But many of the guys
already consider me "short."　That does not refer to physical
stature.　It indicates that you only have a short time left to go on
your sentence.

I was thinking about the unique sense of self that emerges out of a
situation like this when one is cut off from family, friends and other
support systems.　I remember that I have actually had one other
similar experience like this that also effected a major change in my
life's direction.

After I refused induction into the armed services in 1970, I felt
very much cut off from the mainstream of life in my own
country.　That act was the culmination for me of several years of
anger, frustration and alienation.　Not knowing what else to do and
feeling certain of eventual incarceration, I decided to pursue a long-
time dream of traveling in Europe.　The act of refusing induction
was frightening, but not so frightening as the prospect of traveling
alone in a foreign country.　But I intentionally chose to travel alone
as a conscious test of my abilities to sustain myself.

Until that time (I was 24), I felt that I was extremely dependent,
particularly in an emotional sense, upon family and friends.　This,
then, was an effort to break those ties and see where it would lead
me.　Parenthetically, it was also a "dropping out" experience, as it
was very popular at that time to become a hippie and take to the
highways.　In many ways, I date the beginning of my life, perhaps
it's not too dramatic to say rebirth, from the time I refused to enter
the military and decided to take this trip abroad.

I felt very much that I was answering a call, not in the Christian
sense, because I did not yet think in those terms.　To me it had
more of a psychological-mythic sense about it.　I was really into

Jung and Kazantzakis' *Zorba the Greek*. Odysseus and Henry Miller were my mentors. *Catch 22* and Greek tragedy and Bob Dylan formed the parameters of my world view and ethical outlook. As to my political analysis, it was pretty much hardline S. D. S. anti-imperialism, but with a nascent commitment to nonviolence. I had said no to Christianity.

I felt as though I was laying myself open to whatever happened. Breaking out of my safe, sheltered environment, breaking ties with family, friends, the past. It was a trust in some as yet undefined spirit. It was a letting go. Until that time I was afraid of everything that was unfamiliar, unknown, strange. Now I would pit myself against the unknown. In retrospect, it was something of a pilgrimage or more accurately the beginning of a pilgrimage upon which I still journey. In the beginning, it was a pilgrimage into the unknown, requiring all of the feeble faith that I could muster—faith that the unknown would not denounce me; faith that strangers would be kind; faith that it was safe to sleep by the roadside, in city parks and wheat fields; faith in my ability to survive; faith in the goodness and charity of others.

Before I left for Europe, I stopped with a friend in Boston. It was there in a bookstore that the most important event of the trip occurred. I learned how to pray again. This is kind of embarrassing to admit, but I owe my conversion, for that's what I think happened, to an at-the-time popular, though now long forgotten, book on the drug culture. I would rather be able to say that it was Merton or Dorothy Day or St. John of the Cross who brought me back to Christ, but I can't. The name of the book was *Beyond the Drug Experience* by Robert S. de Ropp. Which was pretty much where I was at the time. So it appealed to me when it talked about mantras and meditation. One of the mantras it mentioned was the Jesus Prayer, which I chose for myself possibly because of a latent feeling for Christianity, but more probably because I liked J. D. Salinger's book, *Franny and Zooey*. The book talked about repeating the mantra over and over until it became as natural and unconscious as breathing and every breath was a praising of God. Well, I've never really developed to that level of spirituality, but I immediately grasped the practicality of this style of

85

praying.   If one were constantly occupying one's mind with prayer, it would be easier to combat self-perpetuating anxieties and fears, particularly those associated with being alone.   It also stops the mental tape recordings of scenarios from the past and stupid, repetitious jingles from TV commercials.   All of this was in addition to what I still regarded as the somewhat dubious spiritual value.   So I began to pray constantly.   It was an act of the Holy Spirit.

By the time I got to Europe (it took almost two weeks because I went by way of boat from Iceland), I was so lonely that I was in almost physical pain.   It took about a month before I got used to it.   Though it was an extremely difficult time for me, it was also very good in some of the same ways that it is good to be in jail.   It was a time alone, a time of reflecion and prayer and for many of the same reasons.   I kept a journal then as I do now.

There was a kind of compression and distillation of inner strength, a focusing, a depth of understanding and perception to the point that when I returned home some of my friends simply did not understand me.   I was almost a different person, stronger, more direct, more perceptive and articulate because I spoke from a place within myself.   I think these moments of enlightenment come only very rarely and the insights can be very easily dissipated.   I was fortunate in finding an environment that nurtured these insights.

My coming to the L. A. C. W. was a direct result of this pilgrimage.   After I returned to the U. S., I met a group of young people while hitchhiking back to California.   They took me to a Peacemaker Conference where I met people from the Milwaukee Catholic Worker.   When I returned to L. A., I was visiting my brother at County Jail, when I ran into Jerry Falon who was at the time with the L. A. C. W.   He was handing out free coffee and donuts and—well, anyway, it's a long story.   But everything began with that journey and the point was that there were some similarities to my present experience.

Friday
November 23

Dear Catherine,

Yesterday, we had a big Thanksgiving dinner. It was good, too much sage in the dressing and too much ginger in the pumpkin pie, but everything tasted fine and there was a lot of it. We were given extra time to eat it, and if you liked to smoke there was a big cigar waiting for you as you left the chow hall.

But it was a very sad experience. I wasn't depressed or anything. It was just such a poignant reminder that a celebration is more than just material abundance. Celebration comes from the hearts of the celebrants. It is more than sharing food and drink. It is sharing each other. When there is no community, there is no celebration. To break a dry crust of bread with loved ones is a greater celebration than sharing a banquet with those whose hearts are closed.

This does not mean that community cannot happen among strangers, merely that an atmosphere of oppression and alienation does not readily lend itself to effective community. It was a hollow holiday.

I haven't really come to terms with how I feel about jails in general. When I was younger and a more faithful adherent of anarchism, I was totally opposed to jails and police. As I grow older and recognize my own shortcomings and failings, I am much less critical of the imperfections of our society. I think most people in here probably should be on the streets. About half or more are here for drugs or drug-related crimes. That's a conservative estimate. Certainly I feel the need to remove from society those who commit violent crimes—armed robbery, murder, rape and drunk driving. This is not the environment that I would choose for such people. It only reinforces their alienation, negative self-image, and brings further education in criminal techniques. However, I don't see that the answer is building better jails.

At one time, I thought that the emergence of a utopian classless society wherein the wealth would be equally distributed was the answer. But even in Utopia, there would still be some rules governing basic acceptable modes of human conduct, in other words, laws. Further, there would be sanctions against breaking these rules. The sanctions might be less oppressive, more socially productive, less alienating than the present ones. But ultimately, force would be required and some type of segregation would be necessary for social deviants.

Now don't get me wrong. I don't want you to think that I am a pessimist and deny the efficacy of building new institutions simply because they will also be corrupt. Certainly I think the relative justice of our system could be improved. Along with murderers, rapists, armed robbers and drunk drivers, I would include in the jail population bankers, politicians, military officers, landlords, corporation executives. There I go building more jails which is the beginning of the end of my utopia. We must begin with the recognition that all human justice is arbitrary, relative, imperfect, and tends to reflect the prejudices and power of the ruling elite. We can and should continue to struggle for a more perfect justice, recognizing at all times that we suffer from the same myopia as the rich, powerful and oppressive. We think we are right. It is more important to be humble. Righteousness breeds pride and pride breeds contempt.

We continue to struggle for a more just society knowing that it will not be perfect. Which is why we must stand always with the victims—the poor, the imprisoned, the oppressed. We cannot build the Kingdom. We can only offer a vision, a symbol of the perfection that is to come. The victims are not perfect; once they attain power they become the oppressors.

There I go philosophizing again. I don't even know if what I just said is at all coherent.

There are two doors leading into the chow hall. One at the bottom of the stairs and one at the top. In order to get into the chow hall, one must wait for the deputy sitting in the guard bubble at the end of the hall to open these doors from his electronic control panel. When he "pops" open the first door, there is a sharp crack as if a pistol had been fired. It is echoed and amplified by the cold, hollow emptiness of the stairwell. This sound is immediately followed by the much louder exploding sound of the upper door

blasting through the empty still air.   These two sounds are for me
the very apotheosis of the jailhouse experience.   The icy hollowness
produces a sensation pregnant with dread.

I never really was cut out to be a criminal.   I guess it was my
upbringing.   The depth of my honesty is not nearly so great as my
fear of being caught.   I am basically a "scaredy-cat" and a "kiss-
up," which makes it difficult for me here in jail because the main
occupation is "getting over on the guards."   "Getting over" means
smuggling past the guards anything you're not supposed to have,
which in here is just about everything.   Most everyone is expected
to "play" to some extent.   Well, of course being a "scaredy-cat"
and embarrassed at the prospect of being caught, I would prefer not
to play.   However, I do try to fit into my social milieu.

As I think about it, I am actually much more suited to civil
disobedience than criminal activity.   In c.d. one sets out to get
caught, so there is no fear or embarrassment.

I also give some thought to being a "trustee."   Which means that
I am actively supporting the jail system.   If I were a better anarchist
I would not participate in this form of slave labor.   On the other
hand, Gandhi always said that the civil disobedient should be a
model prisoner and further should gladly accept the lowliest job in
the jail.   In many ways I am not really anti-authoritarian, so the
Gandhian approach appeals to me.

I saw Catherine Bax tonight.   We had a good visit.   But she
seemed surprised when I said that this was the most important work
that I could be doing.   (More on this later.   Have to get this into
the mail.)

Dear Catherine,

Last year at about this time, Kent and Marty and Jon and I were
sitting in a holding tank at County Court.   Kent had just shared a
passage from the Acts of the Apostles.   The Apostles had been
beaten and jailed for repeatedly preaching the Gospel.   When they
were thrown in jail this time the doors were opened by an angel so
that they could return to their preaching.   It was at that time that I
decided to come back to the Convention Center next year.   Actually
I was kind of disappointed in myself for not going back immediately
upon release.   But Kent pointed out that it was the last day of the
convention and it was almost over.   So I allowed him to ease my
conscience with the prospect of returning the next year.   So here I
am and what I want to know is when does the part happen where the
angels come and release us!

To get back to a thought that I was trying to develop last night—I
really am not certain that this is the most important thing that I can
do with my time or if it is going to make any difference in terms of
the arms race.   Perhaps I could be more effective "on the streets"
organizing for next year, speaking, educating, planning, researching,
etc.   On the face of it, it certainly would be a better use of my time
to be at the kitchen caring for the hungry and homeless, helping to
take the load off of other community members (especially Tony at
the bakery!).   I guess the efficacy of an act like this must in great
measure be taken on faith, because we may never know the results of
this act or its effect on human lives and actions.   We do not know if
people will ever be moved by the sight of the Spirit working in our
lives.   Or if the apparent course of history will be even slightly
modified.   It is purely a matter of faith.

But there is one sense of the effectiveness of our actions that has
been verified by personal experience.   On the outside, no matter
what I was doing—community organizing, serving the poor,
demonstrating for peace and justice—it was not enough.   There was
always a subtle feeling of guilt because I was participating even in a

marginal way in a culture of warfare and death. While I have not by any means transcended guilt, I have never been more at peace with myself. To be in jail because of one's commitment to peace, this is the closest I have come so far to a lack of complicity in the crimes of our culture.

The shower stall is filled up with 12 inches of sewage and gets deeper each time someone inadvertently flushes the urinal. The situation is at a precipitously dangerous level and it stinks. It reminds one of a backyard fish pond that doesn't get cleaned often enough.

Last night Catherine Bax was wondering why I continue to be nervous if my living situation and my work situation are pretty stable and the only people who make me really nervous are in other parts of the jail. The distress comes from a lack of control over one's life. I can be moved at any time to less congenial living arrangements. Or, what is more likely, the present situation could easily change at any time from its benign atmosphere to something considerably more dangerous. The people in the cell are constantly changing. All it takes is a couple of crazies to change the balance. I try not to let this worry me too much and accept it as a fact of life. But it is a source of constant anxiety.

Well, enough of this! I haven't said anything about Niebuhr for almost a whole day. So you're probably anxiously awaiting. Don't get worried. This is only going to be a brief discussion (I hope) on a very important topic—the Resurrection of the Body. (To be continued.)

Dear Catherine,

I have regarded the Resurrection as a metaphor for Christian
action in the world.   Whenever we proclaim the values of the
Kingdom through our actions in the world, we, in effect, bring about
a resurrection from a culture of death.   We cause a movement from
the death values of this world to the life values of the Kingdom.   As
to a resurrection after death, I guess I have always rejected that
possibility as rather naive.   My conception has always leaned
towards the more mystical understanding of the Resurrection which
would have the soul reuniting with the vast Oneness of the universe
or re-emerging with the Godhead.

Niebuhr rejects this mystical notion along with two other popular
notions of resurrection—Neo-Platonic dualism and naturalism—in
favor of a more traditional Christian understanding of the
Resurrection of the Body in the Kingdom of God at the end of
time.   I must confess that this notion has never been one that I
could accept, but he is so persuasive in his explanation of the unique
Judeo-Christian acceptance of body-soul unity and the significance
of human actions through which God works towards the fulfillment
of history.

"The idea of the resurrection of the body cannot of course be
literally true.   But neither is any other ideal of fulfillment literally
true.   All of them are symbols of completeness."   The
Resurrection is a symbol of completeness which emphasizes the
importance of body and soul, history and social progress, and
therefore lends great importance to human activity.   Seen in this
light, human history takes on great significance as it moves towards
completeness at the end of time.

Most of us sense something transcendent about ourselves and
define that quality as the soul.   Most Christians perceive themselves
to be working out a personal salvation for this immortal soul.
Niebuhr says that this separation of the corruptible, evil body from
the pure immortal soul comes from the Greek concept of
dualism.   The Hebrews did not distinguish between body and soul

as separate entities.   They located the presence of the soul in the human blood.   There is no such thing as a disincarnate soul.   Body and soul are equal and necessary.   The idea of an immortal soul is no less rational than an immortal body.   Most Christian thought has accepted this notion of dualism, of working out a personal salvation of an individual immortal soul without regard for social process.   Niebuhr affirms the importance of social progress or history.   History is a process of human progress towards a goal of the Kingdom of God at the end of time.   Most Christian religions have rejected the importance of human action and social progress towards a state of greater justice.   This progressive notion of salvation has been left to the Marxists.   But their naturalist view of humanity does not recognize man's and woman's transcendent qualities, which means that we exist for more than mere social progress and Marxism lacks awareness of the depths of humanity's evil.   This means that we are not naturally capable of pure goodness.   There is no natural Utopia.

Niebuhr rejects the simplistic notions of mysticism, dualism and naturalistic social progress.   He embraces the more complex and holistic concept of the Resurrection of the Body as a symbol of humanity's ultimate fulfillment.   This is of course the implication and the promise of the incarnation.

I just saw Catherine and she told me of all of the new crazies who are frequenting the kitchen now.   I had not forgotten how difficult it can be on Skid Row.   But it was brought home to me as I thought of all the past crazies and the fights and the high tensions in the dining room and the long lines stretching farther and farther around the block.

Here at least there are no knives or weapons.   The whole jail was turned upside down in search of a single butcher knife that disappeared from the kitchen.   There are no drugs or alcohol, so people don't do all of the crazy, mindless, violent things they do when they come to Hospitality Kitchen.

When I get homesick and lonely, I try to remember some of the less pleasant things about the Catholic Worker.   It makes me feel better about being here.   After all, it is much easier in many ways to sit here and pretend I am some kind of hero than to live out the daily hardships demanded in a life of service.

Monday
November 26

Dear Catherine,

There is a small group of tiny gnats that swarms each day around the damp, mildewed mop that sits in the corner of our runners' room. Normally, I wouldn't take any notice of such insignificant creatures. But they have become rather important to me in my present situation. Those gnats are the only life form other than male humans that I ever encounter inside these walls; there are no plants, dogs, cats, spiders, trees, grass. Well, the list of nonexistent life forms in this jail is endless. This is the virtual antithesis of life.

Not too dissimilar to the old joke about the guy in prison who spent years training a flea, I have come to a certain appreciation of this nest of gnats. But as in the old joke where the bartender inadvertently kills the trained flea, alas, has my own relationship been so disrupted. Chips, my partner, has taken to spraying our mop each morning with "Airborne Bolt," a bug killer. No longer are my eyes delighted by the playful cavorting and amorous sexual exploits of my nuzzling gnats. And cruelest fate of all, "Airborne Bolt" gives me a sore throat and headache.

Everyone keeps asking me if I am writing a book about my jail experience. Even the deputies are starting to make discreet inquiries. Deputy Winther to another deputy: "Don't ever do anything around here you would be ashamed to get into print." I told him I didn't think this would have too wide a circulation.

"Hey, Johnny. How's it goin', homey?" "Not too good, man. I am goin' back to the pen. Doin' three more years." A casual shrug of the shoulders, "Ain't no big thing."

Some lives are lost forever. No human act can change them. Complete futility. They are perpetual penitents on an endless escalator. Up to the chow hall, down to the cell. From prison to jail. From cage to hell, with an occasional respite in a place called home. But more and more the experience of home becomes foreign to them. Their lives are an endless round of cards and TV, eating and sleeping and shitting and pissing, boredom and belligerence.   Modulated, regulated and institutionalized, these were once human lives, but they died long before they entered this tomb.

Now they walk like zombies in single file, torsos tight and hard, fists clenched, lips curled in a permanent snarl, feeling no pain, or joy, or love or light.   No human lives these.   Spirit and soul long dead.   Body stiff and hard as if in rigor mortis.   These are the perpetual penitents existing in a state of permanent atonement. Like they say: "If you're gonna do the crime, you better be able to do the time."

"Without the cross men are beguiled by what is good in human existence into a false optimism and by what is tragic into despair." (Niebuhr)

Dear Catherine,

Don't relax, don't get comfortable.   This is not a youth camp and
you are on trial at every moment.   You are tacitly tolerated by the
inmates, but don't overstep yourself.   Don't be too jovial.   Don't
overstep yourself.

Oh God, my heart beats like the wings of a sparrow.   Come to
me, make me calm.   I am cold and my body shivers with fright and
insecurity.   Come to me and give me warmth.   My palms are wet
and slimy with moisture.   Save me from drowning in my own
fear.   My back is crooked and bent with tension.   Give me the
strength to stand upright.

I saw Kent today briefly.   He gave me a letter he had written in
response to the copy of my journal he had received.   How I long to
embrace him.   How I long to embrace you all.   There is a deep
and heartrending lack of tenderness in our world.

I didn't feel too much like writing today because that situation
came up that I hoped wouldn't—the one I spoke about in a previous
letter.   I was able to intervene in a very discreet manner, so that
nothing happened.   I don't think there will be any
recriminations.   I hope.   But I did get really nervous.   Even
smoked a cigarette!   I am very tired.

"I was rough and often cynical.   He taught me that roughness
was fear and cynicism was defeat." (Agnes Smedley)

"Do you not see that you work for a lifetime and in the end get
nothing for it except death?   How can you in the face of that speak
of rewards, or choose anything but that which is fundamental and
true, and work for it even if it does not succeed?" (Agnes Smedley)

I hate the chow hall.   It intensifies everything distasteful and
distressing about jail.   It is cold and loveless.   It is glaring enamel
and spotlessly clean.   It is food passed by an anonymous pair of
hands through a small opening in the serving counter.   Not a face,
not a body, just a ghostly pair of hands clad in thin white rubber
gloves.   It is weary eyes casting covert glances over steaming cups of

coffee at long lines of prisoners who march in single file, hands in pockets, staring right back.   It is metal trays, metal cups, metal tables and a single metal spoon.   It is a meal eaten in stony silence or forced jocular conversation with much laughing about women, drugs, fast cars and scamming.   It is eating potatoes and gravy and meat and vegetables and salad and two pieces of bread and milk and coffee and apple pie all in four minutes.   It is the eyes of glaring guards waiting to tap your table and tell you to "pick it up."   It is waiting 20 minutes to get in, 5 minutes to get out, and 15 minutes to get back into the cell.   This is sustenance and survival, without grace, dignity, humanity.   In one orifice and out the other.   Eating or shitting, it makes little difference.   And yet even in the midst of this graceless machinelike process, a moment of hope.

Could that be Marshall, the young black kid with the broad shoulders and bad teeth, who always argues about cards?   Could that be Marshall I see with his head bowed over his metal tray, while all around are shoveling to beat the clock?   Perhaps he is sick and cannot eat.   Maybe he's just not hungry.   Then he makes the sign of the Cross.   In the name of the Father and the Son and the Holy Spirit.   Amen.   And he begins to eat a little behind time, having taken a moment to bless his meal, our meal, the prisoners, the guards, the jail sanctified and dignified in a moment of grace.

Dear Catherine,

PSALM 22

My God, my God, why hast thou
Forsaken me?   Why are thou so far
From helping me, and from
The words of my roaring?

Our fathers trusted in thee: they
Trusted, and thou didst deliver them.

They cried unto thee and were
Delivered.   They trusted in thee and
Were not confounded.

But I am a worm, and no man, a
Reproach of men, and despised of the people.

All they that see me laugh me
To scorn.   They shoot out the lip,
They shake the head saying,

He trusted in the Lord that he
Would deliver him: let him deliver him
Seeing he delighted in him.

But thou art he that
Took me out of the worm: thou
Did'st make me hope when I
Was upon my mother's breast.

Be not far from me, for
Trouble is near; for there
Is none to help.

When I first came to the Catholic Worker I was not very Christian in my world view. I remember I was painting cabinets in an old building over on Glendale Blvd. that was to be converted into a free store. It suddenly occurred to me a divine insight that it really didn't matter what I did, how menial or insignificant the task, as long as I was making a contribution to the Revolution. I wonder if that kind of self-sacrificing attitude would have stayed with me if I had continued to preceive my struggle solely in terms of a revolution, rather than in terms of the Kingdom of Justice? I think not. I would have been ultimately disillusioned.

If I were a criminal, I would promise never, never to break the law again! I would completely reform and change my ways. I would go straight and no longer associate with my criminal friends. The consequences of a life of crime are much too disastrous to justify such actions. I wish I were merely a criminal.

The most important thing that seems to be emerging from this process so far is a recognition of my own arrogance and pride and my lack of trust and humility before the Lord.

Certainly the actions that we took in blocking the entrance to the Convention Center indicated a tremendous sense of righteousness. It is not possible perhaps to assure that that righteousness did not devalue into self-righteousness. Such that we assume ourselves blessed in the eyes of God and our adversaries condemned in the eyes of God. Such judgments are not ours to make. If we do not approach these situations with the utmost humility and recognition of our own participation in the sinfulness of humanity and need for forgiveness, then we stand condemned for self-righteousness.

As we are all the principal protagonists in our own life film or novel or epic poem, we tend to lend too much significance to our own activities, personal creativity and ability to effect change in the world. I stand convicted of this sin of pride and arrogance. This is not to deny that there have been some achievements, some accomplishments in my life, for I am no self-flagellating ascetic. There has simply been a lack of sufficient awareness and acknowledgement that without God I could do nothing. With God all things are possible.

I believed too firmly that I was the author of my own novel, director of my own film. In our work there is a great temptation to self-righteousness. We begin to think that we are the only ones who are doing the Lord's work. We will certainly not ever be accused of hiding our light under a bushel basket. Good God! When we suffer, half of Southern California knows about it. That is not to demean either my suffering or sacrifice, but there are thousands upon thousands who each day silently bear much heavier crosses than I. We must be careful not to wear our crown of thorns too proudly or expose our wounds like compulsive postoperative storytellers.

Dear Catherine,

"So long as our struggle to be present in prayer and nonviolent resistance does not reach the heart of that invisible mass murder, our unused freedom makes us complicit in the ultimate sin against life." (Jim Douglass, *Seattle Times*, Nov.17, 1979)

What frightens me more than being here in jail is the prospect that the successful completion of this event implies a call to even greater personal responsibility and sacrifice for world peace and disarmament. The call can only be answered in the hope that the necessary grace will be forthcoming, because I know that I do not at this moment have the will power and the fortitude and, yes, the deep and abiding faith to carry on such an apparently futile struggle.

I never cease to be amazed at the power that has carried me this far in my life. A life of sacrifice and dedication runs directly counter to my outstanding abilities to survive and my pragmatic urge to turn situations to personal advantage. Witness how capably I manage my relationship with the deputies. I can't help it if I am witty, affable, intelligent and just a natural kiss-up. "Good morning, Sergeant. Have a good weekend. You know we aren't the same without you around here. Not nearly as shipshape." The sergeant kind of brightens up. And I silently kick myself in the ass for being such an obsequious boot-licker. I don't mean to. It's just that I was raised to be polite, pleasant and respectful to those in authority, and I am so good at it. Well, I tell myself I'll try to be less pleasant, not so accommodating to the deputies. "Hi, Jeff! How's it goin'? Why so glum? Anything wrong?" "No, I'm fine, thanks, Deputy Martin." Who does he think he is trying to act friendly to me?

Well, I'll try another tack. I just won't do any work until I am asked. Normally, I just get up and start sweeping or cleaning off the fingerprinting table on my own. Partly because I know it has to be done and I hate to be told what to do and partly because I am just compulsive about doing a good job. I know. I know. It's unreasonable to be compulsive about doing a good job in jail, but

youthful habits are difficult to break.   I just naturally fit right
in.   I'll never make a good revolutionary.

Part of my problem is unconscious reaction-formation.   So
obviously, I am not fully responsible.   But my survival techniques
that I employ with the other inmates are anything but
unconscious.   With the $40 that my father left me, I buy extra
candy and cigarettes.   Now I do share them with those who cannot
afford to buy such things.   But quite often it just so happens that
these recipients of my charity are also among the physically largest
residents of Tank 22.   And further, most of them are of Latin
extraction, with lots and lots of tattoos.   The Latin culture being the
socially dominant force in the jail population, I have made a
concentrated effort to integrate myself through the media of
interracial economic-development grants, loans and outright gifts.   I
have also cultivated an extremely sensitive and sympathetic ear,
listening to endless hours of hard-luck stories, jail stories, drug
stories and broken marriage stories.   The other night several
Chicanos walked by my "rack" saying hello or otherwise pleasantly
acknowledging my presence, prompting one Anglo acquaintance to
remark: "How do you get to know all of those geeks?"   Now you
have to admit that my actions have been pretty blatantly self-serving.

I keep telling myself that I am just trying to get through this
time.   Next time I'll try to overcome my baser survival tactics and
perfect my Christian revolutionary approach to the jail experience.

Last night I witnessed my first fight.   It was downstairs in Tank
21.   It started with a card argument about 9:00.   We could only see
glimpses of it reflected in the glass windows of the guards' catwalk.
Though I couldn't see it, it sounded extremely brutal.   Several
thudding sounds of bone smashing against flesh, then quiet for
almost two minutes, then an explosion of steel beds toppling to
cement floor.   More punches and grunts and "mother-fuckers" and
grunts but not too much shouting as people are shushed and told to
be quiet so that "the man" will not hear what is going on.

"The man" in fact never heard what went on, did not know there
was a fight until the two losers were "rolled up" by the victors.
That is, they were made to roll up their bedrolls and were kicked out

of their cells by the other inmates.   I learned later that though the immediate cause of the fight was a card game, it was actually precipitated by mounting racial tensions in the tank.   The Anglos in this case ruled.

About 20 minutes after the fight was over and we were all once again watching Willy Nelson on TV, "the man" came in force.   About 15 deputies were observed double timing it down the catwalk.   Then there was an announcement: "Tanks 21 and 22, everyone into the dayroom.   Take all of your personal property with you."   It was another shakedown and strip-search that lasted almost three hours.   No one got too much sleep that night.   Apparently they were searching for weapons in anticipation of racial recriminations.

A lot of people were shifted between Tanks 21 and 22, but strangely enough, the various participants in the foray were left together in Tank 21.   Usually the management is much more sensitive about such arrangements.   Nevertheless, things seem to have declined, though I've heard that blacks stay together in a tight group and have not yet ventured into the dayroom again.

Deputy to a new inmate who wanted to make a phone call: "Sit down.   Around here you'll have to learn that patience is not a virtue; it's a necessity!"   Truer words have never been spoken.

Yesterday while serving chow in the hole, I noticed that the prisoner in Cell 328 had refused both lunch and dinner.   When he refused lunch today, it occurred to me that there might possibly be more to this than simple loss of appetite.   "Leave it there for him anyway," the deputy told me.   "I don't want him saying we didn't give him a chance to eat, then filing a writ on us."   When the deputy closed the door, I observed that there was extensive notation on the small card that normally contains only name and booking number.   On the card it said: "Steve Esparza, 357-623.   This is one tough mother-fucker.   He refuses all food and will not accept a bedroll.   He is the former spokesperson of Cell 25."

Chips had heard about him.   He apparently has a bad attitude and his constant filing of writs with the court does not endear him to the management.

In order to explain a very interesting event that took place in our tank on Thursday, I have to describe the layout of our module.   I am in Module D, Tank 22.   There are six tanks in the jail, three on the third floor and three on the fourth floor.   Each module has four tanks, one up and one down.   Running between the tanks is a glass-enclosed catwalk from which the guard can observe activities in the two tanks on either side.   The tanks on one side generally contain 50-70 men, in dorm style.   On the other side are generally 14 single cells, upper and lower, for either protective custody or "high-power" (the tough guys).   Inside the catwalk is a control panel from which the guard can control all doors, lights, etc.

Well, now for my story.   We were just sitting on the bunk when I turned around and looked out of the bars into the glass-enclosed catwalk.   And what did I see but about 25 well-dressed people with little red I.D. badges on, staring right back at me.   All of us were kind of taken aback because the immediate sensation was that here we were in the zoo!

There we were sitting like monkeys in the zoo, while these people stared at us and the guide talked and gestured with his hands and pointed at us.   I think everyone felt much the same way as I did, very humiliated.   One guy was even sitting on the toilet at the time.   Several people had similar thoughts to my own, that we should take down our pants or climb on the bars and swing around like apes.   Everyone acted out these fantasies after the group had left but I think we were all just too stunned to act while they were here.

It's a difficult experience to be in jail, dehumanized, locked down, caged like an animal.   When you are in here you try to lose track of an outside so that the experiences of imprisonment do not stand in such sharp contrast to freedom.   It is cruel to heighten that contrast by displaying our helpless condition as if we were animals.

Friday

November 30

Dear Catherine,

I am feeling much better about being here, though I still feel very
much in God's hands.   Of course, we are always in God's hands,
but for me that was only a vague intellectual concept until I was
arrested.   Not until then did I realize how utterly and completely
we are dependent upon the Lord.

Recently we were interviewed by the *L. A. Times* and Channel 2
News.   At first I didn't want to do the interviews, partly because I
just want to keep a low profile in here and partly because this has
been so deeply and intensely a personal experience that I didn't feel
as though I could share it with the news media.   It would be
sacrilegious.   And besides it wouldn't make good copy.   I only did
the interviews out of a sense of duty to the original cause.   But I
didn't feel as though I did a very good job.   Usually I am very good
at that sort of thing.   I have, over the years, cultivated an intensity
and rhetoric that make good news copy.   This time I found myself
fumbling because the experience I was going through was not
communicable on that level.   They were interested in the conflict
between us and Judge Fitzgerald.   And I had gone beyond
that.   They just were not too concerned about my renewed prayer
life, my new-found humility, my increased perception of the tragedy
of life and its resolution in the Crucifixion and Resurrection of the
Body.

Well, anyway, the article came out today and the TV interview
came on this evening.   In both, I was struck by the fact that though
neither Kent nor I was very eloquent, Judge Fitzgerald sounded
venal, petty and vindictive.   The paradox of a society that punishes
peacemakers while honoring military murderers was vigorously
exposed through no effort of our own.

The other effect of the stories is that my status among both guards
and inmates seems to be significantly improved.   I had forgotten the
power the media have to enhance the importance of a person.   I am
not really all that humble.   I just didn't care that much to be in the

media.   It was the furthest thing from my mind.   I have had the experience many times before so it wasn't unique for me.   I was really surprised at the relatively high degree of interest there was from the entire jail population.

One inmate up in the kitchen, who is always giving me a hard time about my antiwar activities and even threatened to punch me, completely changed his attitude.   He apologized to me profusely for no reason other than I had my picture in the *L. A. Times*.

When we went down to do the TV interview, we had to go outside, another fringe benefit.   The deputy that accompanied us out is a real hard-ass who gives all the inmates a rough time.   But I could tell that he was super impressed by the presence of the TV crew (he got to wear his hat and revolver which made him look quite fearsome) and by our un-eloquent statements.   He even got on camera for a brief moment escorting us back inside the gate.   That should really blow his mind.   After he got back upstairs I saw him talking to about six other deputies.   They had a copy of the *L. A. Times* and I overheard enough to know that they were talking about us.   The power of the press is amazing.   It's 11:00 P.M. now and several people in my tank are watching the late news to see if the story is on again.

Dear Catherine,

The media coverage seems to have been a very positive event for me.   I was feeling relatively smug and confident last night at all the affirming comments I had received.   Then as I was preparing to go to bed, Allen, the older guy who sleeps next to me, leaned over and said, "If I ever needed a friend it's tonight.   I overheard some of those guys in the bathroom saying that they were going to throw water on me after I went to bed."

Oh great!   This guy's in really bad shape if I'm the only one he can rely on for protection.   "You know, these young guys don't like old guys like me.   I was down in Tank 8 a while back and they burned an old guy.   While he was asleep, they crumpled up some newspaper and lighted it and threw it under the blankets.   They woke him up, but he still got a little burned."

I stayed awake and read until most everyone had gone to bed, not really knowing what I'd do if trouble did develop.   I figured that I would just have to rely on my newly established media status and my candy- and cigarette-cultivated relationships to provide support for any sort of counter-action.

Fortunately, nothing happened and I finally went to sleep.   Next morning though I discovered that Allen had "rolled it up."   That is, he had, in the vernacular, gotten his ass out of there.   This is not a completely benign environment.

My bunk, or rack, or pad, is located at the most extremely incommodious terminus of the tank.   It is near the washroom/shower/toilet/TV room area.   So I can plainly hear everything going on on the tube, which is a real advantage if you like always knowing what's on TV.   I am also privy to the loud and rowdy coffee parties which take place near the shower because the improvised toilet-paper stove has a tendency to burst into flames.   Just before you enter the shower area, there is a row of five drinking fountains.   There is a two-foot space in between fountains 1 and 2, indicating that a sink was removed, leaving just exactly

enough space for my bunk.   I am virtually a part of the whole
bathroom scene.   This is a convenience as one does not need to
vacate the bunk in order to quench one's thirst.   The drawback
however is that one is surrounded by all manner of disgusting
bathroom-type activities.   There is always someone trying to talk to
you with an enormous load of toothpaste in his mouth, some of it
dribbling down his chin as he struggles to make himself
understood.   Then there is the inevitable and thoroughly
disconcerting PLOP as the first wad of toothpaste hits the
sink.   This is followed by vigorous rinsing and hacking and perhaps
the dislodging of copious amounts of loose phlegm.   The other
ablutionary activities of shaving and washing are not nearly so
disturbing and in fact produce an atmosphere of relative intimacy.
Just like one big happy family all in the same bathroom.   I guess
this is what happened last night as I laid there between sink 1 and
sink 2, while Tony was brushing his teeth at sink 4.

Tony is our jailhouse barber.   He is tall, about six feet, and
broad-shouldered, with thick black hair combed straight back and
dark Latino good looks.   He has large white teeth and he kind of
keeps them clenched so he sounds like a tough guy when he
talks.   He is your basic tall, quite tough guy and well respected
among all the other tough guys.   His muscular arms and torso are
covered with dark hair that grows to rather an extraordinary length,
and, of course, the inevitable tattoos—a little red impish devil that
looks out of place, a swastika, a skull with a top hat and plenty of
women.

Tony is a pleasant, easy-going guy.   We had never had much of
an extended conversation but I like him.   He always said hello to
me, and he was one of the first people I met here who assured me
that even though I was nervous everything would be O. K. and I
could make it.   About a week after I got there, I found myself in
Tony's barber chair: "Don't worry, man.   You'll be O. K.   After
the first month, the time just slides by.   The secret is don't
worry.   Don't worry about nothin'.   The man always asks me,
'Hey, Tony, how come you got such patience?   You never get mad
at anything.'   Hey, I ain't got no choice!"   I'll continue this
tomorrow.

Dear Catherine,

Tony gave me the best haircut I've had in years but until the other night we hadn't done more than nod at each other. He finished shaving at sink 4 and was just walking past my bed when he turned to me and said: "Hey, I seen you on television. Man, you were good. Just tell that judge to go fuck himself." "Thanks, Tony. I really appreciate the support. A lot of guys in here don't understand that. They think I am crazy." "Well, hell, man, they don't know shit. You might as well just kiss everything you believe in good-bye if you write that letter." "I know that, but everybody in here thinks that the most important thing is just getting out." "Hey, now, well hell, you had no business doin' what you did in the first place. You shoulda just stayed home." "I know, I know!" I said with the enthusiasm of one who after much frustration and despair, has finally found someone in a foreign land who speaks his language.

Tony walked back to his bunk and I lay there reflecting on his uniqueness. Then there he was back again sitting on sink 3, cigarette in hand. "You know, man. I had a similar situation to yours. That's why I ended up doin' five and a half years in the joint." I was a little skeptical that Tony had ever been involved in civil disobedience before, but I was willing to at least listen to his story.

"I was 18 when they sent me to the joint. On a forgery beef— $28.50. I forged a check for $28.50 and they gave me six months to fourteen years. Now if I was somebody, anybody, like if I had money or if I knew somebody, I'da walked. But I am nobody, so I got sent to the pen for six months to fourteen years. I didn't belong in the pen but that's how the system works. If you're somebody, you get cut loose; if you're nobody, you get sent to the pen. It's fucked."

Thinking that there were other factors involved, I asked: "Did you have any priors?" "No, man. I'd never been arrested in my

life." "Were you using drugs?" "No, I didn't start 'slammin''
until I was in the joint." "God, that's incredible that they put you
in jail for so long for $28.50!" "Yea! But I coulda got out in six
months if I'da played their game. After six months, I came up
before the parole board for review. They asked me all these
questions and like I just said: "Fuck you," and walked out of the
room. "What kind of questions did they ask you?" "Oh, they had
a bunch of questions like 'What are your plans for the future? Do
you have any bitterness? Do you have remorse for your crime?'
Do I have any bitterness? Hell, yes, I am bitter. I shouldn't even
be in here on a beef like this!

"I guess that I shouldn'a opened my mouth like that but it was the
truth and I was pissed. You get a parole hearing every six months,
but after that I didn't even bother to go anymore. I just sent 'em a
note telling them that this didn't have anything to do with justice."

When he got out of the pen, Tony was 25 years old. A friend of
his allowed him to take over payments on a Peterbilt truck. "I was
just on the verge of signing an exclusive trucking contract that
would've meant $100,000 a year profit. I had three trucks and eight
people workin' for me. I had a wife, a kid and a pad. I was
makin' it. I had everything. But the more I got, the more
problems I got. I worked hard to get my wife the nice things that
she wanted, but the harder I worked the more she complained that I
was never home. So I finally just gave up! We got a divorce and I
left her everything."

Sometime after the divorce, he was picked up on a petty thievery
rap and spent six months in County Jail. When he got out, he was
arrested again for nonsupport. "I told the judge that I couldn't
make payments because I was in custody at the time. He said, '365
days!' I said, 'Hey, wait a minute. Didn't you hear me? I said I
was in custody at the time!' He gave me two more months for
contempt of court."

At some point in all of this, he was charged with an armed
robbery. I didn't think that it was acceptable to ask him whether or
not he did it. I think he did. Anyway they have offered him nine
years. "I gotta fight it. Otherwise, it's nine years back in the
joint. If I was somebody, they'd cut me loose. But I am just a
nobody."

Dear Catherine,

Two nights ago I saw a fight on television. James Scott was fighting a guy named Yanki Lopez from Stockton, California (Fat City). The unique thing about the fight was that it took place within the walls of Rahway State Prison, a maximum security facility in New Jersey, where Scott is serving a life sentence. The fight was a slaughter from the beginning. I have never seen such a brutal and aggressive match. Clearly, Scott had saved all of his frustration and anger at prison life and viciously released it during his fight. Prison life easily lends itself to a compulsive, disciplined life style. He has absolutely no other distractions. He is completely dedicated to training and fighting, living and breathing for that only.

While I was up on the roof running (two more guys started running today), it occurred to me that if per chance we don't get out on January 17 (God forbid), I would really push to go to Lacey or the farm. It would be easy in one of those places to run for hours and hours. In fact, I could run for as many hours as my body could handle. It would be a terrific time to train for a marathon! Suddenly, the prospect of two more months didn't seem so bad at all. Don't worry. I am not getting to the point where I enjoy this jail life, but the marathon fantasy could certainly sustain me if we found out that we couldn't get out for some reason until late February.

It would almost be like not being in jail because when I wasn't eating, sleeping or working, I'd be running. It would be easy to get in over a hundred miles a week, get plenty of sleep, avoid fattening foods and not drink any beer. What a training program! Absolutely no distractions or responsibilities to interfere with a single-minded goal. And I understand that the farm diet provides unlimited quantities of protein and fresh vegetables. Look out, Michael and Anthony Trafecanty! You better start praying for my early release. Otherwise I am heading for a 2:45 marathon and a 31-minute 10K. Well, it's nice to have fantasies.

Lately, I have had this premonition that we would be getting out of here sooner than we think.   Maybe not, it could be just another fantasy.   While this thought makes me very happy, it also gives me some cause for concern.   There seems to be some process at work within me, a purging, a deep growth in understanding, a separating of the wheat from the chaff.   It is as if an enormous search light has been turned on within me and so much that was obscure is now bathed in light.   I wish with all of my heart to be out of here and reunited with friends and family, but I do not wish to truncate that process.   And further, I fear that the intensity of my realizations and perceptions will diminish considerably when I leave this place.

The experience is much like fasting.   If one does not eat, one is obsessed with food and even the thought of a simple crust of bread produces ecstasy.   But after a few days of normal eating, our sensitivity to the joy, mystery and power of food is diminished. Our senses are inundated by the sheer volume of the possibilities.

So it is with jail.   I know that the joy, mystery and power that I have perceived in the world beyond these walls will quickly recede before the onslaught of daily existence.   I feel such a clarity of vision that, at times, it gives me an almost physical sense of excitement.   This gift of sight is only occasionally imparted to us.   The muddied waters of our life are made clear for a brief instant only to be just as quickly obscured in the tumult and turbulence of our daily lives.   On the basis of that brief insight, we are invited to act.   Do we have the courage to act out our visions?

Last week there was a young man in the hole for about four days who came most clearly to my attention because he was such an anomaly.   Most of the people in the hole at any given time are Chicano.   Probably about 95%.   Mostly they are hard-core tough guys who are relatively stoic about their condition.   Mr. Branstader was another story entirely.   He was a tall, thin guy who distinguished himself by his constant whining and "sniveling." Every time the deputy was around, he complained about being too cold, having nose bleeds and seizures, not getting his medication, going crazy and on and on.   Certainly not your typical tough resident of the hole.

Then one day he wasn't there.   I later found out that he had been transferred to an even deeper hole that I have yet to see but is famous in jailhouse legend—the *Rubber Room*.   The Rubber Room is a padded cell with a hole in the middle for relief of bodily wastes.   No toilet, no sink, no bed.   The prisoner enters without clothes.   It exists primarily for therapeutic purposes, preventing the inordinate from harming themselves.   However, it is apparently used on occasion for purely punitive reasons.   While I thought that Branstader may have been something of a neurotic "mama's boy," his behavior didn't seem to warrant such action.   One day I finally asked Chips how such a guy like that ended up here, much less in the hole.   "Didn't you know that Branstader is charged with murdering his mother?"

Dear Catherine,

While I was at work today, one of the other inmates walking by asked me if I was going to write the letter to the judge.   When I said no, he responded, much to my surprise, by saying, "Good!" "Thank you.   I really appreciate your encouragement."   "I seen that guy on TV.   He was coppin' out, backin' down all over the place.   'They wouldn't even take a lawyer or try to fight it.'   He was pretending like he had nothin' to do with it.   Like it wasn't even his fault that he gave you six months.   If I was you, every night when I got in bed I would say, 'Fuck that judge!' "

Kent saw the public defender last night.   The news was stunning, to say the least.   I quote from Kent: "Our every prayer has been answered.   First, Judge Fitzgerald is planning to modify our sentence.   He seems likely to let us out before Christmas.   Second, he wants us to be at Lacey (always has).   He wrote an angry letter to the sheriffs telling them we should be there.   Third (and now for the biggie!!), he is feeling pressure—not only from the outside, but from within.   The lawyer thinks that he is losing sleep, and she has noticed a change in him that she never thought possible.   He seems confused and more humble—his sentencing of those convicted has taken a marked change.   He is more open to the public defenders' suggestions.   The lawyer can't believe it.   She would have thought it impossible.   The judge admits that six months is too much time and feels painted into a corner.   He would love for us to make any gesture of compromise—*any* request for a shorter sentence.   I told her that I did not feel ready to do that at this time.   (The pressure he feels is good, I believe.   I see no need to let him off the hook.   Not that I would cause him any pain.   But it seems creative, as though the more he feels it, the more he will be transformed.   Our every day in here is a problem for him.)   He has been apparently deeply affected by the more than 500 letters he has received (has read most, if not all).   Some that caused the greatest change of heart were those from the National Riflemen's Association supporting his hard stand.   Jeff, a miracle is taking place.   And we may be out of here soon!''

And so the ice is thawing, the dawn begins to break at the end of a long night.   Will we remember while standing in the warm sunlight, surrounded by friends, perhaps even acclaimed by some, that by our own feeble efforts, nothing was accomplished?   It is only through the grace of God that we have survived.   If indeed there is any triumph this belongs to the Lord alone.   If we could only become as humble servants whose wills are completely attuned to the will of God, great things can be accomplished.   We must wait upon the Lord.   This is the lesson I have only just begun to learn in this place.   We are such forgetful, willful beings, I fear that this lesson will be too early lost.

Dear Catherine,

I was lying peacefully in bed last night feeling pretty good about the day's events, just getting settled in for a long night of reading, maybe eat a candy bar or two, when the deputy called me out for a visit in the A-B building.   Oh shit, I thought, a long wait in a tiny cage and then after that a search, and then after that a wait outside my mod door.   But maybe it's that public defender who talked to Kent.   It might be worth it to talk with her.   When I got down, I asked the deputy if he could tell me who it is (just checking to make sure it's not a priest or minister).   "It's a lawyer, Dietrich.   What d'ya expect?   TV reporters?"

Anyway not to make a long story out of this, the guy was a concerned young liberal lawyer from Laguna Beach, named Kenny.   He had walked in the candlelight vigil and was concerned about us.   So he went to Judge Fitzgerald on our behalf.   The judge was open to any suggestion.   Kenny's proposal was that the judge allow us the right to go back to the Convention Center next year but we would promise not to break the law.   I was pissed because I knew I had to wait up to two hours in the cage after this visit and this guy had brought me the same old story.   I tried to be a little nice but when he said there are better ways to accomplish our goals than by breaking the law, I got disgusted.   "What if everyone did what we did?"   "We stopped the war in Vietnam through the system," he said.   "Not until thousands of people spent a lot of years in jail and hundreds of thousands died," I shot back.   I was too pissed to have a very reasonable dialogue with him, so I am sure that I confirmed an image of an arrogant nonviolent terrorist.

Dear Catherine,

I think I am in paradise.   This can't be jail.   There is green grass
and trees and flowers.   Cars passing by and tall buildings confirm
an impression that people still exist who are neither prisoners nor
guards.

I didn't expect to be transferred today.   They told me it would be
Thursday.   So it was a surprise when they told me to "roll it up" at
7:00 this morning.   I had to change into my street clothes for the
transfer process.   It felt good to put on my own clothes, almost like
I was going home.   As we drove away I took a final look back.
This would not be the last contest and the opponent had not been
defeated by any means.   But it was at least a known quantity
now.   This jail is a crucible in which the metal of the spirit is
continually tested.   I would be back.

Compared with the main jail, this place is a summer camp—trees,
shrubs, grass, baseball, horseshoes and a track!   You won't believe
this.   I don't believe it either, but I was able to talk them into
letting me keep my running shoes!   I said that I needed them for
my back.   I made a silent pact with God that if he would let me
keep my running shoes, I'd stop bothering him for a while.   I think
you are not supposed to ask for such things.   But I consider running
a spiritual exercise.   Look out, Michael and Anthony!

I am working in the kitchen which means less time for reading and
writing but it feels like home to be back working in a kitchen.   I also
have access to all of the fresh fruit and vegetables I can eat.   I am
trying to stay off the carbos.

The main drawback to this place is that the administration is
totally into a military mentality.   Fold your clothes just so, make the
bed with the corners tucked in, get a haircut, call the guards
"sir."   A lot of bullshit, but we don't see the guards too often and
the guy in charge of the kitchen is cool.   All of the inmates are very
cool.   No one "walks that walk or talks that talk."   The best
feature, however, is no TV in the barracks.   It's very quiet and

everyone has to go to bed at 9:00. Great !

Being here is like being in summer camp. You can call off the
pressure on the judge. I am ready to start full-time training for
another marathon. I can't believe I have my running shoes. God
is good.

My body feels as though I have been crying for a long time. And
now my tears have ceased but there is a residual pain and fatigue that
yet remains. A great burden has been lifted.

A fresh evening breeze blows into the barracks. It is cool and
smells of grass and flowers. I can hear the sounds of rushing traffic
and see the lights of the city. Will I always be so conscious of the
great gift of life that God gives to us?

Dear Catherine,

I feel deeply this sense of brokenness.   A great burden is
lifted.   An incredible tension is diminished.   But out of this
brokenness, this shattering, so much has surfaced that was hidden.

Right now I feel a little cut off from people on the outside, because
I didn't get a chance to talk to anyone before the transfer and the
mail that I have gotten doesn't acknowledge that I am in here,
because it was sent to me before I got here.

Boy, they do make you pay dearly for the privilege of being
here.   I am still trying to get the work routine down.   I like the
kitchen but it's a long day.   We serve every meal seven days a week,
and we also prepare two meals a day.   We alternate one day cooking
breakfast (3:30 A.M.) and lunch.   Next day, dinner.   So it's not a
solid block of time.   I am always running back and forth between
the dorm and the kitchen, not always knowing exactly where I am
supposed to be.

I still haven't figured out the proper manner of folding my clothes
and making my bunk.   They actually hold daily military-style
inspections and they give demerits if you fuck up on anything,
including not folding your clothes or making your bunk
properly.   There is an incredible amount of military-style bullshit
and the majority of the deputies seem to enjoy it too much.   I really
wonder how healthy a person who enjoys this kind of mildly sadistic
anality could be.   I feel absurd and demeaned as a person to be
required to spend such an inordinate amount of time on folding my
clothes properly.   There was something dramatic about being
locked down in the main jail.   It was a challenge and a struggle.
Here they can kill the spirit with insipidness and tedium.

I understand that the farm is not like this at all.   It is much more
relaxed, probably due to the rural setting and removal from constant
inspection by officials.   Apparently, the farm is the Hilton of the jail
system and Lacey is the Motel 6.

I do miss Kent. Though I hardly ever got to talk to him, it was heartening to see him every day. I can't believe the way everyone seems to overrate us. They thought we were going to organize demonstrations in jail. What a joke! It was all we could do just to survive.

Well, so much for the bad news. The good news is that I have about five hours a day free for running! I am trying to restrain myself. I don't want to overdo it. Today I ran for an hour and exercised for an hour—situps, stretching, etc. Then I took a shower. It was great!

Another good thing for everyone is that, as you can see, I now have a pen.

The facility is right next to the county dog pound. Many of the inmates work at the pound caring for and feeding the dogs and destroying them when their time comes and removing the carcasses when they are dead. At various times during the day and night, the dogs begin to bark, crying out their fear and anguish and their desire to run free. Strangely, their human counterparts remain silent.

Friday
December 7

Dear Catherine,

This place is the PITS!   Today, for the first time, I really wanted
out.   I felt defeated, almost reduced to tears.   I was overwrought
with tension, paranoia, and frustration.   My stomach was tied in
knots.   All because of the tedious, absurd and superfluous rules
here.   I don't know if I am going to make it!
I am not generally a paranoid person, but that seems to be my
general attitude about the guards here.   There are only a few of
them, but by their overbearing, supercilious, military demeanor, they
make their presence felt.   The guards at the main jail were generally
more relaxed.   In fact, I felt almost sympathetic towards them.
After all, they too were locked down in the jail just as surely as any of
the prisoners.   Perhaps because we were so securely behind bars,
they felt more comfortable about being human at times.   There
seemed to be an understanding that if you didn't fuck with them,
they didn't fuck with you.   There was a realization that the inmates
were as low as a human could get, so why make the situation worse?
My paranoia stems from the fact that here the administration
seems to make a deliberate effort to ensure that you will not enjoy the
minimal privileges afforded by the facility.   Each morning they hold
inspection to make sure that each bunk is properly made and clothes
are properly folded.   I must have spent almost two hours learning
the process and finally doing it.   After a certain point, I felt absurd
and degraded by the amount of precious time that I had wasted on
such a superfluous and meaningless project.   I just said, "Fuck
it!   That has got to be good enough because to spend more time on
making my bunk and folding my clothes has got to be a sin."   So I
was really upset after having spent all this time on the project, plus
endless hours of worry, to find when I got back from work that I got
two demerit marks.   How demeaning!   Like some high school
kid.   I almost cried from embarrassment, anger, frustration.
If I get one more demerit mark, which seems very likely, then no

visits next week.   Five demerits in one week, no visits, no
commissary.   Ten in one week and you are in the hole.   How
absurd to be sent to the hole because you can't get the blankets to
fold around the corners of your bunk at 45-degree angles.   The only
thing I am really concerned about is visiting privileges and that's the
first to go.   If I can make it through Sunday without getting
another demerit mark, I still retain my visiting privileges.   But it's
pretty clear that I probably will not be able to make it.   I think a lot
of people here end up without visits.

So I am ready to come home anytime.   This is the first time that
I have felt anger at anyone in the whole process.   This place grates
on me.   It is insipid and insulting punishment not suited for a
recalcitrant child, much less a full-grown adult.

Needless to say, I have lost a lot of focus and inward reflection.
In many ways, much of the somewhat dubious benefit of this process
has been severely undermined.   Today I have felt more like
throwing in the towel than at any other time.   Because I feel
physically safe and secure, I have lost the intense need for a close
relationship with God.   I have gone back to automatic pilot.   But
in many ways this place is much more dangerous to the spirit than
the main jail.

I am still running and that's good.   But that could also be what
got me in trouble.   Apparently, the inspection of my bunk was
going O.K. until the deputies noticed my shoes.   How come I need
tennis shoes for a bad back?   If I needed them for my back, why
didn't I have them on?   If I had a bad back, why was I spending
hours every day running?   I wasn't able to answer these questions
because I wasn't there.   Well, I try to keep a low profile.   On the
whole, it's still better here, but I don't know how long I can handle
it.   Keep praying for me.   The environment is better, but it is no
easier.

I wish Catherine were coming tomorrow and not Sunday.   I
really feel out of contact.

Hey!   I just thought, it was Fitzgerald who got me in here.   I
wonder if he would send me out to the farm?   Someone go ask

him! Get me outta here!!

Disregard the last paragraph. I'll write him myself if it doesn't get any better.

I wish that I hadn't heard that we were being released early. Now every day I think maybe this is the day. I dread the prospect of going back to court. I hope we can get out of here without that.

Dear Catherine,

I forgot to get stamps and envelopes today and I haven't received
more in the mail.   They may not allow anything to come in the
mail; it is so-o-o petty here.   I tried to stock up on anything I might
need from the commissary because it is highly likely that I will get
five demerits and not be able to buy anything.

This could be my last letter.   Oh, wait.   I just remembered I
bought four packs of cigarettes to give away.   I still have one left
that I could trade for a couple of stamps.

I feel a little better, but still very oppressed by the environment.
The administration of "justice" is so arbitrary.   The dorm
housekeeper keeps the place clean and stands inspection when the
deputy comes each morning.   He said the deputy gave someone a
demerit for being a troublemaker, didn't even look at his bunk or his
locker.   Moral: Don't get on anyone's shit list.

During visits today, the inmate in the bunk next to me had the
experience of having his visit cut in half when the deputies asked his
visitor to step into the gate house whereupon they promptly arrested
and handcuffed him, taking him to County Jail for traffic
warrants.   Apparently, they check the drivers' licenses as visitors
come in.   This particular visitor looked "suspicious," so they kept
his license and, unbeknownst to him, ran a warrant check on
him.   How venal and unfair.   It is a galling and embittering
experience.   It cannot but create a diminished sense of respect for
oneself and anger at authority figures.

I have started to pray more and that seems to help.   But this
place makes me impatient to get out!   I wish the public defender
had not told us that we might get out soon.   Now every time they
announce releases, I think it might be me.   There is nothing worse
than false hopes for a prisoner.   It is a thousand disappointments a
day.   Better no hope than a false one.

I run all the time when I am not working.   I try to run myself
into oblivion, into unconsciousness.   I try to run off my frustration

and anger.   As I run, I pray.   Lord God, have mercy on me.
Lord God, forgive me.   Give me peace and joy and strength.   Not
my will, but thy will be done.   I run until my head is light, almost
floating, my body is pulsating and tingling from blood and air
rushing to every cell and corpuscle.   I run until there is no tension
in my stomach and the salt sea sweat stings my eyes and soaks my
shirt.   Until my body and my mind are purged and my spirit leaps
easily over prison walls and barbed wire and, free, runs down the
riverbed to the sea.

At night I sleep easily.   Tomorrow I have to get up at 3:00 A.M. to
make breakfast.   Hotcakes.   It will take all of my will power not to
eat some.

The dorm is quiet right now because everyone is at the movie.
How blessed!   The silence is broken only by the periodic blast of
the P.A. system.   It is turned up much too high, so every time it
comes on, I just about jump out of my skin.   I lose my breath and
my heart skips a beat.   The voice coming over the speaker is always
distorted because the speaker system isn't designed to be turned up
so loud.   This not-so-subtle form of torture makes it almost
impossible to sleep during any time except after lights out.   Every
time I hear it, I feel the urge to flip off whoever is speaking.

Oh, well.   It is better than the 24-hour TV torture at the main
jail.   Except that this is so much more deliberate that I take it very
personally.   There is no getting around it—this is definitely what is
known as a "chicken shit outfit."

At night I hear the sound of the freeway.   Ordinarily so repulsive
to me, it now sounds so joyous and free.

Sunday

December 9

Dear Catherine,

It is really hard for me to write.   I feel in such a turmoil and a
quandary.   I really don't like it here, but I am not too excited about
going back to the main jail.   Certainly, I seem to have lost the sense
of inner peace and focus that I had in the other place.   Now I feel
intense anger and tension and frustration.   I am such a coward.
Dare I squander a fortune for a little physical safety and a few
creature comforts?   Perhaps it is better to be caged up like some
animal than to be free like Pavlov's dogs.   I know if I just straight
out request a transfer, the administration, in fact everyone, will think
I am absolutely crazy.

I was so ashamed today when Catherine Bax and Catherine Morris
came for a visit.   All I could do is complain.   I hadn't realized how
much this had gotten to me.   Usually, visits are a real joyful time
for me.   But I had no joy for them, only anger.

There almost seems to be a kind of dignity to being locked down as
opposed to paying for privileges with your active cooperation.
Pretty soon they not only have the body but the soul too.

I am not the hero type at all.   My original intention had been to
do the easiest time I could get.   When I think about going back to
the jail, it seems so stupid.   I was thinking today that above all we
must be human.   Sometimes being human means that we are
infinitely tender and compassionate, and at other times it means that
we are strong, immovable, unyielding.   We must struggle to be
human.   If I could just wish myself back where I was, I would do
it.   It is the process of doing it that intimidates me.   It's like
getting arrested all over again.

Today while I was running, I thought of my brother, Joe.   I
think of him often while in jail because I am always seeing young
guys in here that remind me of him.   Yesterday my mother spoke of
seeing him in cuffs and leg-irons being brought into court.   He did
some time in L.A. County and at Atoscadero.   In 1972, he died in

an apparent suicide.   There had been many previous attempts.   I guess, like everyone who is associated with a suicide, I felt extreme pain and guilt.   It was most particularly intense since I was the last one to see him.   Even now my heart is heavy and my eyes begin to sting as I write this.

My brother had many problems and I think I was the last one he could turn to.   He came to stay at the Catholic Worker to help out for a week or so.   When the time was up, I suggested that I could give him a ride home.   I could tell that he really didn't want to go.   But it was an incredibly awkward and extremely intense time at the Worker.   No one seemed to fit in, least of all my brother with his emotional problems as apparent as a bleeding wound.   So I drove him home, but he didn't really have a home.   He had no money and no place to stay.   He said he was going to walk to a friend's house and to just let him out on the corner near the freeway exit.   That was the last time I saw him, walking down the street.   The next morning my mother called: "Joe was hit by a truck.   He's in St. Joseph's Hospital.   He's hurt very badly."

Joe was dead when I got to the hospital.   The nurse took me to a special waiting room where my parents were.   They were both crying.   My father was much more shaken.   Of the two, my mother seemed the stronger.   When the doctor came in, he offered his sympathies and asked if we wished to see the body.   Oh God, no!   I thought.   I just can't.   I can't look at my brother's body all torn up.   Hit by a truckload of coffins right across from the Pilgrimage Theater on the Hollywood Freeway.

My mother went in alone.   Dad and I stayed together in the waiting room, neither of us having the courage to take a last look.   I knew at the time that I would regret not going in with my mother, but I just couldn't.   When we left, the nurse gave me a brown plastic trash liner filled with what was left of my brother's worldly possessions.   I put them in the back of our old brown Plymouth station wagon, where they stayed for two weeks, and followed my parents home.

There is an image of my brother that came to my today in the midst of my anger and frustration.   While he was in County Jail,

they sent him out to the farm in Saugus.   At one point, he grabbed
the hose attached to one of those upright gasoline tanks that you see
so often in rural areas.   He sprayed a circle of gasoline around
himself and the tank.   Then he lit it with a match.   To me, that
was rage personified.   A ring of fire.   I see my brother with his
pent-up, inarticulate rage trying to blow himself into oblivion.

Dear Catherine,

I woke up two hours ago, feeling very good, very well rested, my mind clear. The reveille call at 5:00 A.M. is extremely obnoxious. It is a whining siren sound that reaches higher and higher intensity. I hate it, but I remember back at the jail in one of the cells that I was in, they would open and close the automatic doors simultaneously on 24 cells, slamming, clanging, banging them, until they were satisfied that everyone was awake.

Today I am trying to remember all of the bad things about the jail, in order to make an accurate assessment of both places. This morning I feel good. I'll see how I feel by evening. If I can just continue to do my own time and not let the agenda of the place pervade my consciousness. I am willing to put in a reasonable amount of time on the required superfluous activities. If that isn't good enough, then that's O.K. I am going to try to be detached about the loss of privileges and try not to play their game. I really played right into their hands this last week because I was so concerned about securing my visits, and also I am by nature a very cooperative, hard-working person who responds very well to a reward system. How unusual! Aren't we all trained to respond well to that kind of system?

If I can only purge this anger from my heart and not let it destroy the sense of inner peace that has developed. If I can rid myself of this tension and paranoia and not care what the guards do (they are after all not causing me any harm; I am the one who allows them to take over my consciousness). If I can continue to give what I consider a reasonable amount of cooperation and not concern myself with the consequences. If I can stop my rabbit heart from leaping every time the always gruff voice barks out a command, then perhaps I can stay here.

I know by now that you have written to the judge. But I have decided not to write to him. I feel that if I can't make it here, I can very easily have myself sent back to the main jail. Perhaps it will be just the logical consequence of the attitude that I am trying to develop. I am sorry for the ambivalence that I have expressed to you, both in this letter and in our visits.

It has been very difficult to work out my feelings about this place. Furthermore, I just reread my letter to the judge and it sounds so whining and sniveling that I cannot bear to send it. If this place continues to shrivel my spirit, the most reasonable thing to do is to go back to the main jail, which does not require an order from the judge.

If I am still here, I will be more cheerful at our next visit. If I cannot be more cheerful, then I will be back in jail.

Catherine, I love you so much. Even though I didn't show it at our last meeting. How I longed to walk out of here and go with you and Bax to my brother's restaurant. But this time of separation has been good. It has made me realize even more how important you are to me and what a gift our life together is. What we have is so rare and precious, and yet as strong as a rock. Only God can give such gifts. I thank him every day.

Dear Catherine,

I was in bed early and sure enough: "Dietrich, report to the gate house!" Oh shit, now what? Everything had gone pretty well today. I got in three hours of running. No one hassled me. Not so bad. Now what?

As it happened, it was good news. Lisa, the public defender, was there. Looks like the judge is going to let us out for Christmas! Yipe! The bad news is that they strip-searched me afterwards. Not exactly standard procedure, I understand. Boy, it sure makes me paranoid. I don't know what they think I am going to do. I kept thinking this is really humiliating and degrading. But I saw an image of Christ stripped by his executioners. Seen in that light, it is something else again.

Lisa, the lawyer, repeated pretty much what the other lawyer had said to Kent—that the judge had really changed. He was losing sleep at night over this whole thing. He has even changed his opinion concerning the arms race itself. Lisa said that the judge was going to bring us to his chambers on the 24th of December to give us a Christmas present. She assumes that the Christmas present is to be our release. In addition, she thinks he wishes to make some kind of monetary donation to the Catholic Worker.

That's really great, but the question that comes to my mind is that if he has had such a change of heart, why doesn't he just release us right now?

Tuesday

December 11

Dear Catherine,

Every day here is a struggle.   Am I cooperating too much in my own imprisonment?   Am I compromising too much for comfort and safety?   A totally different kind of struggle all together from the other place.   Yesterday was not too bad, not good at all, but not too bad.   Sometimes I feel guilty about running and enjoying it because such a simple pleasure can make it too easy to stay here.   One day at a time.   Oh God, I need you now more then ever.   Running and praying, I think constant thoughts of freedom.

They called my to the gate house about 15 minutes ago.   I still jump when I hear my name called.   It was Fran Cooper.   We were just starting to have a visit when the sergeant came in.   He wanted to see some identification.   Fran gave him her business card. "Anybody can have a business card printed up," he said.   "Don't you have something else?"   He wanted to see some ordination papers.   As if anyone carries ordination papers around with them.   Our visit was cut short.

It all seems so picky and arbitrary.   One deputy says yes; the sergeant says no and, baby, you ain't got nothing to say.   Like last night.   Why did they have to strip-search me?   They were watching much more closely than when I had visits on weekends.

Well, on the brighter side of things, I had a job change.   I think that it will work out much better.   I am doing pots and pans.   I come in three times a day for a little over an hour.   It's less work time, more time for running and reading and writing.   I have three to four hours in the morning and the same in the afternoon.   Also, I don't have to serve the line which is a drag.   Everybody complaining, asking for more, the chef telling you to give less.   And sometimes the guys serving have picked out a particular person whom they all decide to short on the food because he has violated some obscure jailhouse code.

Work is good.   The deputies in charge of the kitchen are very

kind and compassionate.   Cooking, however, was a bit of a
drag.   They did most of the cooking.   The prep work was done by
someone else entirely.   My job was just to stand by and listen to the
deputies talk about their lives, their service careers, sports, marriage
and on and on.   Oh, and maybe I would open a few cans or mop the
floor.   But that was it.

Now I have my own area in the back of the kitchen and I just
come in, do my work, clean up my area and leave.   Most of the time
I am at work or on the field.   I am at this moment at the far, not too
far, south fence line next to the freeway.

I do a lot of running.   I am going to try to do four hours
today.   I try to avoid as much as possible any contact with the
administration.   I know there are harsh rules and attitudes at the
County Jail.   I don't know why this harshness seems so crushing
here.

Last night I woke up about 2:30 A.M. and couldn't go back to sleep
because of an unresolved tension about the unnecessary strip-search.
I had run for three hours the day before, so I had expected to sleep
until morning.   Today I will try running for four hours and see
what happens.   Maybe I can't run it off.   I do a lot of praying.   I
pray for strength and patience and love and joy.   Most of all, there
is no joy here.   What are trees and grass and birds and flowers
without joy?   I pray also for the deputies, that they may understand
that these are human beings here.   Because a man commits a crime,
he is not less than human.   I suppose that I should be thankful that
the guards are not brutal.   There is not even a hint of physical abuse
or even a racist attitude as there was at the main jail.   But clearly,
prisoners are not regarded as completely human.   At first I thought
that the intention of the administration was to instill fear in the
hearts of the inmates so that they simply did not cause any
trouble.   Now I think that it goes a little deeper.

Today while sitting on the field, a fellow prisoner mentioned
rehabilitation.   When you first come in the deputies talk about

giving you a job that matches your job on the streets. The cook in the kitchen is always going on about providing you with skills in food service. Learning respect for those in authority, learning responsibility by making your bunk and folding your clothes neatly, learning discipline by getting up on time, going to work and getting to bed early, good grooming habits—these are essential and are also required. You won't see any slovenly long hair or scraggly beards around here or dirty clothes or dirty fingernails either.

Perhaps this is what provides the deputies with their almost evangelical righteousness, their sense of mission. I don't really know but that kind of outlook would certainly provide a great deal of justification for any personal misgivings. Though I doubt that any of them ever has misgivings. But a sense of mission combined with control over "subhumans" is a powerful combination that is extremely destructive, as we saw in Nazi Germany.

The other possible intent of this place is to make it as miserable as possible as a deterrent to further criminal activities. In any case, whatever the intention, I would guess that this place is a failure in that it probably doesn't prevent recidivism and certainly does not build good citizens, much less good, sharing, compassionate, responsible human beings. I venture to say that most people leave this institution feeling extreme anger. The pettiness of the routine must create a distaste for any self-discipline.

I keep a running tab on the guards' behavior. They scored one yesterday with the search and one today by cutting off the visit with Fran. Maybe I can make it through the rest of today with no other scores. I am just trying to keep control of the tension. So far, it's O. K. Just writing about it makes me feel better and gives more clarity to my thoughts. Running helps. But it is a day-by-day thing. I am so glad that they kept Kent and me at the main jail for so long. If they had sent me here first, I think they might have broken me. I would really have been jumping and constantly depressed at being here, but fearful of the threat of going to the main. So I don't want to go back, but if their score gets too high, I'll not be afraid to return.

134

Catherine, I just got your Sunday-Monday letter. I would like very much to see you alone. Is Lisa going to ask about a transfer to the farm for me? Is March 2 our new release date? Oh boy. If we don't get out on December 24, then I definitely would like to get to the farm. It's 5:30 now. Just as I was writing, I got called to the gate house—score two—just checking to see if I got a haircut as per instructions last night. Well, tomorrow is another bright new day! I'll try again. I love you and I miss you.

Wednesday

December 12

Dear Catherine,

I try to walk straight and tall, not hunched over like a prisoner. I try
to smile, not scowl like a prisoner. I pray for patience and joy. I
think those are the gifts of the Holy Spirit. Aren't there seven of
them? I don't remember, but I think fortitude and long-suffering
must be among them. It occurred to me this morning that I should
pray to the Holy Spirit. Most of all, I must pray for joy. The sky is
clear and blue and cloudless after last night's wind. The mountains
with their silent message of fortitude and eternal endurance are
visible. A small leafless sapling tree entwines its uppermost
branches in a straggly embrace with the barbed-wire fence. If we
have no joy, we are lifeless, barren creatures. With joy we purge
our hearts of anger. With joy we open our eyes to the beauty of
God's creation.

Oh Lord, I surrender my life to you. Into your hands I put my
whole self. Whatever cross you send I know that you will give me
the grace to bear it. I have no hope. My hope is in the Lord. I
have no expectations but that the Lord will give to me the fortitude
to bear all hardships and trials. I ask only that you give me joy in
place of my anger, fortitude in place of my weakness. That the
tears I shed will wash my heart clean and make my eyes truly see. I
am a man who has no hope except in the Lord's mercy. Though
they despise me and revile me, I will not reject you, Lord. Though
my heart breaks from loneliness, I will yet remain faithful. In my
pain and loneliness, my tears and desperation, I will yet remain
firm. Though I am broken and empty, I pray that this brokenness
is but an open door, this emptiness but an invitation. Come, Lord
Jesus. Comfort me in this, my hour of need. Grant that my tears
be tears of joy. Bind these wounds and make me whole once
again. Oh God, if I should fall from your loving hands, I would
shatter. Protect me, oh Lord. I beg of you.

This is the prayer I write as tears keep flowing. This is the
appropriate prayer for this season of Advent. Oh, come Lord Jesus

Christ.   Give us joy and peace.   Hasten the coming of your
kingdom.   For the tears I shed are not for myself alone.   I feel
deeply now, in the midst of my own pain, the suffering of the broken
and despairing.   Despairing to the point of global suicide.   I feel
the pain of the hungry and war-torn, the loneliness of the prisoner in
the hole.   Oh, come Lord Jesus that we might sit as brothers and
sisters around your table.

Dorothy Day said once that the only prayers God answers are
those said in tears.   I have not cried since my brother Joe died, until
today.

There is a place deep within us that can be found only in the
moments of our most utter despair and pain.   From that place of
truth that surpasses all understanding we see our lives in perspective.

Today I am unutterably miserable.   For the first time I could not
bear being in jail any longer.   I felt my only hope lay in the judge
letting us out early.   I was hanging by my fingernails, gritting my
teeth.   I can only make it a few more weeks.   Then after that, I
just won't be able to stay in here until March 2.   I began to believe
that the fate of my life hung on the whims of a mere man.   Then I
began to pray in my misery.   Oh Lord Jesus Christ, come to
me.   My life is in your hands.   Without you I do not exist.   I am
beaten and humbled.   No matter what they do to me, I beg of you,
stay with me.   Then the tears began to flow and I could not stop
them.   Strangely, I feel better.   Whatever happens is God's
will.   My life is completely in his hands.

Catherine, your last letter was very helpful.   I also appreciate
your sacrifice of fasting.   I hope that you will break your fast before
you get here for our visit.

Dear Catherine,

The tension seems to be gone. The struggle is over. Now everything is in *God's* hands. How we must struggle to learn that. We can do nothing, nothing, until we allow God to work through us. Then all things are possible.

Thursday

December 13

Dear Catherine,

This is a letter to Nancy and Anne.   I thought you might like to
see it.   I was happy to see in the *Times* that we are to be released on
the 24th.   Now it is a matter of patience.   I love you and miss you
as if a part of me had been cut away.   I am doing fine.   Keep
praying for me.   I still need it.   I think the meeting in the judge's
chambers on the 24th will be trying.   I have a feeling that there may
be a lot of media there.   This could be the Christmas story of
Southern California!   I hope we are up to it.   You should start
planning for a Christmas Eve Mass of peace and thanksgiving.   I
am looking forward to seeing you.

I love you and I can hardly wait until we are together again!

Dear Nancy and Anne,

I know that it must be rather strange to think of your brother in
jail.   Certainly it could be a source of embarrassment to you.   That
is why I am writing—to explain why I have chosen to go to jail and
sacrifice my freedom and happiness.   Sometimes freedom and
happiness are not the most important things in the world.   If we
believe in something deeply enough, we may be willing to sacrifice
these gifts.

You know I believe that God wants all men to live together in
peace.   This was the message of Christ—peace on earth, good will
towards all men and women.   But you remember that Christ was
arrested and sacrificed his very life for this principle.   Christ was
crucified because people live by fear and greed and cannot accept the
message of love in their lives.   We are always so fearful that an
enemy will attack us and take our wealth that we cannot believe God
will protect us if we would lay down our weapons and give our lives
to him.

I am firmly convinced that the next war will destroy the entire
planet.   I believe that only God can prevent this horrible event from

happening.   But God has chosen to work through human beings in this world.   I feel that it was God who asked me to bring the message of peace to the Anaheim Convention Center Weapons Exhibit by breaking the law and preventing people from entering the building to carry on the business of selling instruments of death.   I feel that God has asked us to sacrifice our freedom and happiness so that through our suffering we might touch the lives of people whose hearts have hardened to God's message of love and peace.

So I ask that you not be embarrassed at my being in jail.   I ask instead that you even be proud that I am in jail.   After all, Christ himself was in prison as were St. Paul, John the Baptist, and many, many of the early Christians.   If we are going to try to be faithful to Christ's message, then we must be willing to sacrifice everything when he asks us—our freedom, our happiness, yes, even our lives, if necessary.

It is possible that the judge will release us before Christmas. Nothing could make me happier than to spend Christmas with you and the rest of the family as we have done every year.   But should it happen that I am not released, then I will consider the sacrifice of my freedom and happiness as a Christmas present to you, my family, the world.

It is not easy for me to be in jail, so please pray that I will continue to have the strength to do whatever God asks of me.   Also pray that God will touch the hearts of men and women throughout the world, so that they will be open to his message of peace and love.

All my love and peace,

Jeff

P.S. I just read in the *L.A. Times* that the judge is to let us go!

Dear Catherine,

"In this our age of infamy, man's choice is but to be a tyrant,
traitor, prisoner; no other choice has he." (Pushkin)

It is so appropriate that we should be in prison during Advent—
this time of hope for the coming of peace, the coming of freedom.   I
have felt a lightness, almost carefree, since today.   Yesterday was a
breakthrough.   I can smile, I can reach out to others who are in
greater need than I.

We can see so clearly that only through suffering will hearts ever
soften.   The world will not be saved through education or
legislation or right thinking, but only through suffering.

It was exciting to read of our pending release in the *Times*. I would
have missed it if one of the guys hadn't told me about it.

Dear Catherine,

I am impatient to be released.   Oh God, keep me close to you;
these last loveless days are the hardest.   I do not know why we must
wait 10 more days to be released.   God must have some reason.
So I continually pray: Not my will but thy will be done,
Oh Lord.   Each day is a struggle and through him each day is a
victory.

December 24th—Christmas Eve.   Once again, if I were the
director of this film, I would fire the writer.   It's just too pat, too
corny.   We could just wind the whole thing up in a neat little 90-
minute film.   All we need for the perfect Hollywood ending is for
someone to announce that the Arms Bazaar will not return to
Anaheim next year.   The last shot will be the whole cast gathered
together at Mass with the two protagonists.   One of the young men
gives a stirring speech about a life dedicated to the struggle for
peace.   He takes a sip from the cup and passes it on.   Camera
tracks back to a full shot of the entire cast as they break into a
moving chorus of "We shall overcome."   Fade out into credits with
music still playing.   The End.

It will never play.   Too corny.   This kind of script went out with
Mickey Rooney and the Andy Hardy movies.   We couldn't even get
World Wide pictures to touch it.

I keep trying to concentrate on joy.   I pray for joy to lift my
spirits.   I beg for joy to unshackle this prisoner's heart.

On Monday my prayers were answered in a manner of speaking.
On Monday Sonny came into our lives.   Sonny invaded the kitchen,
the dorm, the jailhouse itself.   He touched our drudgery-filled,
loveless lives and filled them with joy and jive talk and song, quiet
and bluesy like Ray Charles, most appropriate to our present
environment.   Wherever Sonny is, he fills the room with his
presence.   He is a giant of a black man, six feet five inches high,
with arms bigger than most people's thighs and a chest like a 50-
gallon drum.   At 40 years old, he is a little past his prime, his gut
sags a little and his pectoral muscles have drooped into small

tits.   But he is still a large, powerful man.   His laugh is loud and his smile a yard long.   Though he is always talking about his life and his experiences, I feel that he is deferential and considerate of others, not at all the braggadocio street dude that we so often encounter in our work.   On his right arm is an amateur tattoo.   It says, "Mr. Clean, quiet and mean."   "My partner put that on me while we were doing time in the South Island brig.   Toughest brig in the whole Marine Corps.   I ain't never seen nothin' like it. Makes this place look like a Sunday school.   I used to shave my head so I looked like a black Mr. Clean.   That's why my buddy put it on there.

"Joined the Marines when I was 16.   I started young."

(Apparently he started young in a number of areas.)   I got nine kids and sixteen grand-kids.   Not all by the same woman, of course.   It was four different women.   Messes a woman up to have too many kids.   Sure enough.   It does."   Now that's what I call a considerate man.

Sonny said that at one point in his life he used to be a con man. "You know, the three-piece suit and briefcase number, where they thank you for takin' their money.   None of this strong-arm shit."   I can certainly believe that.   After the first 10 minutes in the kitchen, he was running the place.   The deputy in charge was taking orders from Sonny as he whipped up some "Louisiana stew."   "You ain't got any oregano.   Man, you gotta have oregano.   It brings out the flavor.   This stew gonna make your mama cry.   You ain't never gonna wanta go home again.   This ain't no jailhouse stew.   I put my feet in this stew.   It got soul, man."

Everyone in the kitchen heard over and over that his stew was something special, and soon the word spread quickly throughout the jail, until we had 10% more than expected for dinner.   Sonny served the stew and sang its praises to each and every inmate.   "This ain't no jailhouse stew.   I cooked this stew.   Here lemme get you some meat."   I tasted it myself.   It was O.K., nothing special.   But such an aura had been created by Sonny that people were actually coming up afterwards and thanking him and complimenting the stew.

One day while looking at his enormous arms, I asked Sonny if he had ever been a fighter. "Oh sure. I was Battalion Champion in the Marine Corps." Sonny still makes his way by virtue of his physical prowess. "My last job? I owned my own collection agency. Now don't get me wrong. I didn't go after the small flakes. I only bought accounts of over $25,000. It was a pretty good living. I just tell the flakes that I have an 85% collection rate. I don't threaten them. That's against the law. I just tell them that I don't go to court. But I always collect. The ones that don't pay don't have the money."

The thing that I most appreciate Sonny for is that he rescued us from the dreaded "Gang of Three." I also call them "Los Tres de Barracks." They are recent graduates from the Orange County Youth Authority camps, where they majored in the three R's— rowdiness, rudeness and roughness. They have decided to do their postgraduate studies here at the Theo. Lacey Institute. Every evening they practice their lessons in a very loud and unruly manner here in our barracks, disturbing the otherwise tranquil environment. No one really wanted to challenge them because it meant taking on three at once. On his first night here, Sonny was very tired, so he just said, "Hey man, pipe down. Some people have to get up at 3:00." Total silence. I watched the whole scene, smiling inwardly, looking out from under my blankets like a little gnome. "And justice shall triumph." Generally the barracks has been calm ever since, except when Sonny takes a shower and sings "Cryin' Time."

Dear Catherine,

I just finished my journal entry and mailed it. Went to take a shower. Standing under the hot stream of water, my body felt rejuvenated. Sonny's strong baritone bouncing off the white tile wall, he sings a concert of songs for me: "Moonlight in Vermont," "Stardust," "Misty," all of the old big-band songs. What a rare gift to be standing naked in the shower next to this great bear of a black man listening to his beautiful voice, while steam swirled around us and the water beat on our bodies. I felt such a sense of brotherhood. "Oh sure. Music is my life. I sing at all of the local clubs around here. But here, this is my theme song: 'Mama may have, Papa may have, but God bless the child who has his own!' You know, that's true. When you got it, everybody is your friend. But when you ain't got it, nobody is your friend."

Sonny just got dressed in his blues and splashed on some after-shave before going "out on the town." That means you are going to watch TV. Before he went, he just gave me the most incredible lecture on his philosophy of life, for about 45 minutes. I won't give you all the details. It was basically that if people are fuckin' with you, then you be nice to them until they figure out that they are being assholes. "Like when the deputies start pushin' me around, saying do this, do that, I just say yes sir and run and do it and then I ask 'em what else they want me to do. They expect me to rebel and when I don't they just stop messin' with me. It's the same thing with that judge. If you hadda yelled at him and called him an asshole, he woulda kept you in here. But you didn't. You were just nice and quiet and took it and just gave him time to think about what an asshole he was being."

Dear Catherine,

I read in the paper that Judge Fitzgerald said, "I didn't think they would be as stubborn as I am." I think that we are not stubborn but faithful. There is a difference. Stubbornness is our own will. Faithfulness is God's will.

I was thinking today as Catherine was describing the typical hassles of a Catholic Worker winter scene that in a sense to be here in jail has been a privilege. It has really been a time away. Completely away. It has been a time of reflection and strengthening of faith and a rededication. It is so different from the other times that I have spent away from the Worker. Usually when I am on a vacation, the longer I am away, the less I want to come back. I begin to feel sorry for myself because I am missing a lot of middle-class privileges. I feel less committed to the Worker the longer I am away. But being here has made me feel stronger and stronger about the things that we are committed to. Though I don't look forward to the usual winter hassles, I am excited about coming back. I think people have been putting out to take up the slack. I am anxious to get back so that others can relax a little. Of course, I'll have to play the modest hero role a little. Only enough so that I cannot be accused of false humility.

My time is going easy now. It was really difficult as I began to get "short." That's jail talk for getting close to your release date. It is a strange phenomenon, but the shorter you get the more difficult it is to do your time. When I thought I had six months to do, I would just think of today and the next day. Or sometimes I would think about a date that was close like the end of the first 30 days. But I would try never to think of six months because the sheer weight of the time would oppress me. Now it seems as though it doesn't matter whether it is six months or six days. Anytime you try to swallow the whole package all at once it will weigh you down. So I am back to one day at a time.

I have a good routine now and that makes it go even easier. In order to avoid the three reveille sirens that wake people up (I should say jar people abruptly out of sleep as if their heads had been ripped off), I have gotten one of the kitchen people to wake me at 4:15 A.M. Reveille is at 5:00. I get over to the kitchen by 4:30. No books are allowed so I just sit there with a cup of coffee and write. No one seems to mind that. At 5:30 I do a little work. At 6:30 is kitchen staff breakfast. They are very good but I try to avoid them. Too many carbos. But I ate very light today so that I can treat myself tomorrow—French toast, eggs, bacon, cereal with real milk and bananas. Pig-out time! At 7:00 I go back to the dorm and make my bunk and fix my box. I have finally mastered the arcane mysteries of the bunk and the box and have not received a single demerit. Aren't you proud of me? At 7:30, return to the kitchen, finish up a few pots. At 8:00, out to the field. I take a book and writing materials with me. I usually read or write until 9:00, then run and exercise for two hours. 11:00—lunch time—I have a big salad. At 11:30, back to the dorm; they count noses. 12:00 is lunch time for the rest of the jail. I wash pots until 1:00 or 1:30. Then out to the field again and repeat morning activities. I run 3-4 hours a day in work boots. They got my running shoes. However, the boots are strengthening my legs. 4:00 is dinner—big salad and a piece of meat. Sounds Spartan, huh? 4:30—mail call. At 4:45, back to work. By 6:00 or 6:15, I am in the dorm. I usually read and write until lights out at 9:00. Not bad. I get to do a lot of the things I like to do but I think it makes me stand out. No one else runs 3-4 hours a day.

Dear Catherine,

At Mass: "Where had he squandered the capital of his morning
spirit?" (Solzhenitsyn)

It was the first time that I had been to Mass in two months.   It
was good to receive Communion, to worship God together with the
other prisoners, mostly Chicanos.   The readings touched me deeply
and made me cry.   The reading from Paul was particularly
appropriate: "Rejoice in the Lord always and again I say rejoice . . .
The Lord is at hand.   Be careful for nothing; but in everything by
prayer and supplication with thanksgiving let your requests be made
known unto God.   And the Peace which passeth all understanding,
shall keep your hearts and minds through Christ Jesus."

And from John the Baptist we heard: "He that hath two coats, let
him impart to him that hath none, and he that hath meat, let him do
likewise . . .   I indeed baptize with water, but one mightier than I
cometh, the strap of whose sandal I am not worthy to unloose: he
shall baptize you with the Holy Spirit and with fire: whose fan is in
his hand and he will thoroughly purge his floor, and will gather the
wheat into his garner; but the chaff he will burn with fire
unquenchable."

The sermon was O. K. but not a winner.   Gotta give the guy
credit, he did try at least to communicate with us.   It wasn't just
priestly garbly-gook, pseudo-theology, pious religiosity, that passeth
for thoughtful communication.   He spoke of sharing our "coats" by
reaching out to the other inmates around us and sharing, inviting
them into our lives.   This was good but then he went into the wheat
and the chaff routine and got a little on the judgmental side.   "If we
are going to be Christians, we can't be running scams on others, or
pulling phony real estate deals, or driving when drunk.   We have to
separate the wheat from the chaff which is the phony excuses in our
lives," he said.

I think a priest should reserve those kinds of judgments for the
Confessional.   It's good advice.   But as I looked around the room,

I saw a lot of men who didn't need to hear that kind of self-righteousness. Some were in on bum raps having done nothing at all. Some had received a year for nonsupport because they had no money and no jobs. Some were alcoholics who need something more than advice from the pulpit. I certainly didn't appreciate the advice. There was no sensitivity to the fact that Christ came with a special message to the poor and oppressed who populate our jails. They are Christ's special people. Those who are in jails and prisons, no matter what they have done, are closer to the Kingdom than any priest, no matter how pious he is. Christ is always with the poor, the suffering, the imprisoned, and they stand in perpetual judgment of our inability to live by Christ's teachings.

I certainly would have interpreted the judgment of the wheat and the chaff in a completely different manner. Those who are in jails and prisons are already in the garner, though they may not know this or believe it or even care. But because they have lost all hope, because they have been rejected by all men as unfit for the world, God has gathered them into his Kingdom. It was a special privilege to worship with these criminals. To receive the body of Christ, to hear the Gospel, to recite the familiar ritual that I have known since childhood. I felt great comfort, I felt at home, I felt at peace.

I am struck by the fact that the intensity of my relationship with God is already passing. I am saddened by this. But perhaps the human spirit cannot burn so brightly forever. Perhaps we must be sustained by the near memory of the light. As St. Paul said: "Now we see as through a glass darkly. Then shall we see clearly."

Henceforth all things in my life will be subject to the memory of the light that I have experienced during this time in jail.

Dear Catherine,

Each new day is a victory.   Each new day a challenge and a
joyous struggle.   I feel stronger than I have ever felt before.   On a
purely personal level, this has been such an emptying process.   One
thing only remains to be confronted.   I pray for the courage to face
this thing in truth.   I pray constantly that truth will guide me for
this is what I have found within.   After stripping and stripping
away layer after layer, at the core is God—the light of truth.   It is
what I have called that cold hard place—where we are totally alone,
totally empty, totally dependent upon God.   It dispels fear and
weakness.   It sees all things clearly, risks all for this alone: the
Truth.

I almost fear what awaits me beyond these walls, beyond this
barbed wire.   Oh God, I pray, let me walk in humility and
truth.   This only do I know.   This only have I learned: Risk all
things for the truth.   Risk love, happiness, security and public
esteem.   Nothing else matters but the truth.   We cannot know the
truth except in humility.

Dear Catherine,

I like the mornings best. There is a newness, a freshness about the morning, and it feels good to have put another day behind. I can't believe that I get up at 4:00 in the morning! But it's no hassle at all. I fall asleep exhausted at 8:00 P.M., so that's eight hours sleep. I feel good when I wake up. Others are still sleeping when I go into the bathroom to shave. From out of the bathroom window I can see the neon cross atop Rev. Schuler's Skyscraper Church. As distasteful as that place is to me, the cross glowing in the dark morning sky remains yet a symbol of hope. The stars are brighter than I have ever seen them in the city as I run through the chilled morning air to the warmth of the kitchen. I stand for awhile, with steaming cup of coffee in hand, in front of the oven, like a cat soaking up the sensuous heat on my sore muscles.

After I have gotten enough heat, I sit down and write for an hour until I have to start work. Today, however, I was informed of a new rule. No writing in the kitchen. Well, I suspected as much. I might be able to stretch it out a few more days because the person who so informed me will not be working mornings again until Thursday. And on Thursday I will be more discreet. Possibly it will have faded from his memory or my own.

Anyway, I wasn't too disappointed because I was trying to write a letter to Dorothy Day and I never feel quite up to the task. I always feel like somehow I don't quite measure up to the Catholic Worker tradition. And after all, what could I say to her that someone else hasn't said before . . . I admire you so much. You are such an example to me. You have changed my life. If it hadn't been for the Catholic Worker . . . Well, I'll think of something.

It has occurred to me that what has happened to me in the last two months might be described as a peak experience. I feel as if I am at a plateau in my life. So much has come together, so much has been

discarded.   There is a feeling of having gotten down close to the
essence.   From this point, I can look out on my past life and see
how all things converge, fit together, make sense, have worked
towards this moment.   I have not quite reconciled this concept with
the Christian concept of *metanoia*.   I certainly have experienced a
profound change, a turning around.   But this does not lead me to
repudiate my past.   On the contrary, as I look out over my past life,
I feel like embracing and confirming it, even those aspects which
traditional moralists might judge as sinful.   Because each incident,
each experience was a step in the direction which brought me to this
perfect moment in time, at least as perfect as any moment in time can
be.

I have been wondering what is going to happen on the 24th.
There are several opinions on the process of going to court.   One is
that you are sent over to the main jail, held in holding tanks until the
bus takes everyone to court and then you spend the rest of the day
sitting on the cement floor until you are summoned for your five
minutes in court.   If you are released, you repeat the process in
reverse, ending up back here somewhere around 7:00 P.M., at which
time they might release you immediately or wait awhile.

The other scenario is not quite as involved but equally
distasteful.   In this one you are called to the control module at 5:30
A.M. and held in the hole for several hours until the bus comes to
transport you to court.   Repeat the scene in the basement of the
court house.   One, however, still returns here for a not so early or
speedy release.

While walking back to the barracks meditating on these unhappy
thoughts, I encountered Sonny.   "Hey man, you are gettin' real
short.   You are so short you could stumble over that cigarette
butt!"   He was not referring to my physical stature but to the
brevity of my remaining time in jail.   I am a "short-timer," albeit a
conditional short-timer.   When I explained my concerns to him,
Sonny said, "H-e-e-ey man, they are going to dress you in your *own*
clothes and take you to da court and release you from there!
Elsewise they never woulda printed all that shit in the papers.   You
the man of the hour.   You gonna be a hero, man!   Trust me.   I

know.   Trust me!"

I like Sonny's scenario the best.   I'll stick with that one for awhile.   By the way, Sonny has transferred out of the kitchen, so he isn't in our barracks any longer, alas.   "Los Tres de Barracks" have been joined by an equally rowdy comrade-in-arms.   I now call them "Los Cuatro de la Cocina" since we all work in the kitchen together.

Ugh!   I blew my training program this evening—eight peanut butter cookies.   They weren't even very good.   In fact, now they feel like lead.   Oh, remorse.   I'll be shitting lead for two days now.   We have a new baker, which is a mixed blessing.   He is much freer with the goodies, but they are not very good.

I hope someone is really getting into planning this December 24th liturgy.   It's not often we get to celebrate, dare I say, a victory.   It is not often that we see the power of God manifested so clearly.   So let's make the most of it.   Lots of emotional songs.   I insist that we sing "We Shall Overcome," and please, no schlocky Christian songs.   I guess some Christmas carols would be appropriate.   In addition to the traditional readings, I suggest something from Kent's letters or my journal.   Make it real soppy, make it emotional.   I don't want to see a dry eye in the house.   Try to invite as many people as you can who expressed concern about us.   This could be a good organizing/consciousness-raising event.

Dear Catherine,

A college education is not a sure ticket to success in our society, but it does seem to be an insurance against failure. "Do not stop, do not go to jail—collect your $200." Here, even more than at the main jail, I am aware of the relatively low I. Q. and educational levels of the inmates. Yesterday, I used the word "preservation" in connection with meat. One of "Los Cuatro" commented that I sure used a lot of big words. And had I been to college? Was I a teacher or a lawyer? In the main jail there was a subtle hostility towards me from some whenever I let a word slip by that they did not understand. I made a strenuous effort to tone down the level of my vocabulary in order to placate people. But here there is no hostility, rather an open awe and admiration. People are always asking me for information on subjects ranging from foreign policy to biology. And of course, most people are disturbed when they discover that I have a degree. "You should be a teacher or something, man," they say. Even the inmates know that people with college educations do not go to jail.

It seems like we could find a better means of dealing with the undereducated and less gifted members of our society than putting them in jail.

JUST SAW KENT! Kent came in on the truck from the farm with a load of eggs. He looked great! Sunburned and lean, the best he has ever looked. As usual, there was an awkward silence between us, neither of us knowing where to begin, trying to choose our topics judiciously in the light of our limited time. Trying not to open the floodgates of our mutual experience, knowing that we could not halt the onslaught of words and emotions. We embraced in the back parking lot for the first time since our arrest. Embracing is taboo at the main jail. We had about 20 minutes to visit. It was uplifting.

Didn't sleep too well last night—too many peanut butter cookies. Can't you just see a reporter asking me about my most difficult experience in jail and me replying, "The night I was tortured by peanut butter cookies." That doesn't sound too hard core, does it?

As I lay awake last night, I looked around at the bunks full of sleeping men. The only sound other than snoring was the squeaking of bed springs like a hundred small animals tortured in the night. There is even now after two months such a sense of unreality. I still cannot believe I am in jail. But it gave me a feeling of peace, even accomplishment. I prayed, "Thank you, God, for bringing me here."

I am reading Solzhenitsyn's *One Day in the Life of Ivan Denisovich*. I tried to read something light after I finished *Cancer Ward*, but it seemed so frivolous and such a waste of time. I wonder why I am so conscious of not wasting time in here when there is such an abundance of it.

What a great service Solzhenitsyn has done for the world by bringing to light the tragic suffering of the Russian people. Clearly Solzhenitsyn would not be too happy with my position of naive nonviolence in the face of such massive suffering and injustice. However, I could not help but identify somewhat with Ivan Denisovich. Though the unspeakable inhumanity of those forced-labor camps makes this place look like a Y. M. C. A. day camp, all jails have some similarity. Ivan spoke of the harsh reveille sound of a railroad tie strung on end being struck by a hammer. The electronic reveille sound here is no less harsh. He spoke of choosing which guard would be more relatively compassionate. It is no different here. Some guards are more human than others. Yesterday, when I got kicked out of the medic's office because I had not signed up for sick call the previous evening, I could not but reflect that Ivan had experienced the exact situation. As I was standing by the warm oven at 5:00 A.M. eating a bowl of oatmeal, I thought of Ivan eating his cold gruel and seeking refuge from the subzero temperature around a wood-burning stove.

Here there is no cold, no beatings. We are dressed well; we eat well; we are warm. But the deputies regard us as less than human; we have no control over our physical lives; and we are but slave laborers for the state. The endless harrassment and searches, the stripping of clothes, the stripping of dignity, the prodding of alien hands. Can we ever be human again? Jails are jails. Some things are the same the world around.

I was telling Kent that what we do in our daily work at the Catholic Worker is the "harsh and dreadful" aspect of our lives. It is the daily, mundane, thankless job of caring for the broken and suffering lives that come to us. It is the frustration and anger that arises from knowing that there is damn little we can really do. It is washing dishes, cooking food, cleaning toilets, and listening to troubled tales when we cannot avoid it. What we are involved in now is not harsh and dreadful, it is high drama. When we suffer, hundreds perhaps thousands (if you count the readers of the *L. A. Times*) react to our every wince, our every grimace. We have been given the opportunity to play out archetypal roles, thereby creating really great theater out of our lives. We are operating on an intensely rarified level of existence, rather far from the mundane world. There are many in this very jail who are more innocent than we are. They have committed only the crime of ignorance or poverty. Yet not one single person watches or even cares. They will serve out their full term, drain completely the cup of bitterness, eat to the last morsel the bread of affliction. Their lives will never be vindicated in this world and no human judge will show them mercy. Theirs is the quiet crucifixion, the silent suffering, that will redeem the world.

You know, what I just wrote sounds pretty eloquent. Honestly, sometimes I don't feel like I am writing this. Today Kent was quoting several things that I had written. I couldn't remember any of them. I kept saying, "I said that? I don't remember writing that." What he quoted sounded pretty eloquent and profound. It'll be interesting reading this thing when I get home. Kent said that it should be published. Wouldn't that be the final irony of this whole experience? To defy the deliberate purposelessness of jail punishment by transforming it into a meaningful accomplishment. Oh, but there we go again, now we not only suffer on TV, in the newspapers, but in book form as well! Movie rights, anyone? Not too many people get as much mileage out of jail as we have. The hand of God is clearly present here.

It is not too difficult to see the profound logic of Gandhi in always asking for the maximum sentence for his civil disobedience actions. If Judge Fitzgerald had just given us 30 days, or even the 60 that we ended up serving anyway, there would have been no concern generated around this whole thing. People would have forgotten about us. We owe a lot to the judge.

Dear Catherine,

I can't believe that it's December 20th already. My how time flies when you're having fun!

I've been thinking a lot about *Resistance and Contemplation*. I don't know what form Jim Douglass's contemplation takes, in fact I don't think his book even mentions a particular method. The term "contemplation" is used simply to describe the spiritual side of our lives which must be an integral part of our resistance. But that concept caused such discord within our community in the past because many people thought we should be taking more time off so that individuals could go on personal retreats. Perhaps that's what Jim had in mind, but I know that neither retreat nor vacation, nor "time off but not away" could ever have produced the profound contemplative experience that I have had here in jail. Even a pilgrimage to Thomas Merton's grave would not be so effective. But I am sure that I am prejudiced. Even now the purely contemplative life-style holds no appeal for me. Possibly it lacks the intensity of this crash-course contemplation. I think that I lack the personal discipline, even the desire and motivation for that kind of life. Even in a monastery, I could find things to distract me from my relationship with the Lord. But here there are few distractions and the need for that relationship is deep, so immediate, so essential, there can be no question of abandoning it. It is the very breath of life. It is more essential than food, drink or companionship. No vacation, no time off, no retreat could ever impart to me such a vision of my complete dependence upon God. I have never had such a feeling of peace, fulfillment, satisfaction with myself.

You're not going to believe this one. I hardly believe it myself. About three days ago, I got, among other things, a mailing from the Migrant Ministry. The deputy passing out the mail looked at the newsletter. I was certain he would not give it to me as such items are strictly forbidden. He handed it to me saying, "Maybe you know my cousin, Arnold Erickson. He lives up north in Berkeley. He's high up in that antinuclear stuff." Well, that was a little shocking, but today I was sitting under a tree reading *The Nature and Destiny of Man* when this same deputy came up to me and said, "You remember I told you about my cousin? He met you and your wife at the Catholic Worker up north last year." Then he said, "Did you get the *Agitator* yet?" I was blown away.

"I saw it, but didn't really get a chance to read it." "Well, I'll give it to you at mail call tonight. I don't know if you're supposed to have one, I didn't ask." "I'll be discreet," I said. "If they catch you, just say I gave it to you."

A crack in the ice, praise God. Boy, am I looking forward to reading the ol' *Agitator*.

I just read my "Letters from County Jail" in the *Agitator*. In all modesty, the kid sounds pretty good. I almost had myself in tears.

CITY HALL
LOS ANGELES, CALIFORNIA 90012
(213) 485-3311

OFFICE OF THE MAYOR

TOM BRADLEY
MAYOR

GRACE MONTAÑEZ DAVIS
DEPUTY MAYOR

December 13, 1979

Judge Robert Fitzgerald
North Orange County Municipal Court
1275 North Berkeley
Fullerton, California 92632

Dear Judge Fitzgerald:

I am writing on behalf of Robert J. Dietrich, who was recently sentenced in your court (along with Kenton T. Hoffman) to six months in jail for participating in a peaceful protest against the military technology show at the Anaheim Convention Center.

Mr. Dietrich is a very socially concerned pacifist who has devoted his life to helping people. During the day he has been working at the Hospitality Kitchen, where 400 to 600 free meals are served daily to people living in the Central City. He serves as the President of the Board of Directors of the Skid Row Development Corporation, and I have appointed Mr. Dietrich to the Skid Row Task Force and the Central City Advisory Committee. These organizations analyze conditions in the downtown area and make recommendations for assisting the residents and upgrading the environment for persons visiting and working there.

Mr. Dietrich is a courageous man willing to put himself on the line in order to make a difference in the world. Peaceful dissent is essential in a democracy where the right to express a minority and/or currently unpopular viewpoint must be protected. While equality under the law may necessitate that dissenters pay the price for breaking the law, a six-month jail sentence seems unduly harsh in this instance. Both Dietrich and Hoffman are obviously no threat to anyone. On the contrary, the many people in the Skid Row area assisted daily by their good works are also being made to suffer by these harsh jail sentences.

I would respectfully suggest that the interest of justice might best be served by a lighter sentence that would not deprive the community of the much-needed services of Mr. Dietrich and Mr. Hoffman.

Sincerely,

Tom Bradley

MAYOR

TB: ml

161

Afterword

Reading these letters brings to mind a painting I once saw, or more properly, the title of the painting, 'The Persistence of Memory.' True memory, which is to say the truest part of ourselves, is persistent in a way that these letters both illumine and chasten. The writing sets in motion a spiritual force that disallows the destructive luxury of moral amnesia.

The struggle of a young prisoner to retain, in the cacophany and chaos of jail, a sense of why he is there, what convictions brought him there, what manner of conducting himself makes sense to his own soul—all this is to me a very epiphany of remembrance. The prisoner bonds his spirit with the great spirits of the past, of the present, of a sorrowfully stuck future—with all those who, for a like mettlesomeness of soul, get themselves locked into jails.

From this point of view, the crime of the author is precisely that he chooses to remember. He is arrested for possession, so to speak, of a dangerous weapon: the spirit. His weapon is memory. His memory forbids the great refusal. He refuses, that is to say, to forget—who he is, where he comes from, what his task in the world is, what traditions, symbols, sacred beliefs, community ideals and ikons press on him. Such a refusal, in a culture dedicated to instant forgetting, is of course misdemeaning, if not positively felonious.

And yet, what other hope can we conjure up, except that such spirits keep on keeping on, remembering on behalf of the race of forgetters? It is a work of stubborn insistence: untimely, clumsy, despised. It is also consequential, in the strict sense. The one who remembers must be thrust away in the hope that he, too, and his damnable bad news may slip from common memory.

The task is one of intercession, advocacy, mediation. These are its noble names in classical theology. The remembering prisoner (who must also struggle lest his message be lost to himself) is thus in the ironic and humiliated position of a last hope. He knows a secret, at once despised and feared. He must be put away so that his world can go on with stopped ears.

I think of a prisoner, of prisoners around the world, of those I love in prison, all that race of precious humans, whom the mad world cannot cope with, whom the mad world cannot, in truth, do without.   How well we do to honor them, whom the world cruelly dishonors, to listen, to treasure their presence, their absence even, to make connection in the universal burnout, with their unquenched conscience.

An image persists, as I read and ponder these letters.   I think of a faithful beast who has witnessed the murder of its master. After keening and howling awhile, the animal races to the village to seek help.   He is dumb; his discomfort, his restless fever are misread, ignored.   The villagers shake him off; some of them mutter about an animal gone mad, nudging about as he does, howling, running here and there, shoving people about.   For a long time his bad news, tragic news, cannot be conveyed or decoded.   Then it dawns on someone, probably a child, a person attuned to nature; something is wrong.   This one cuts loose, follows the dog racing madly ahead.

We know the rest, what they come on, how murder will out.   And through what means—a decision, a separating out.   Required are one or two sensate beings, even with their helplessness.   But also, and compensating for all, their persistence and drive.

Our prisoners are like that: powerless, shoved aside.   But the best of them, how patient, how morally coherent!   How they harp on one theme we would like forgotten—the murders being planned even now, in the warrens and bunkers and laboratories, where the morally insane pay their dues to the gods of death.

In the light of these letters, there occurs to me another sort of letter that arrived in my hands some months ago.   It was written by the overseer of one by the aforesaid laboratories in New York.   As we long since learned, the specialty of the house is research in laser beam warfare on behalf of the Pentagon.   Many of us have been arrested in that place, many times, also for sins of remembrance.

On one occasion we wrote the chief of staff, inviting him to meet with us to discuss his work—and ours.   His response began coolly enough, a certain detached courtesy.   But its mood darkened; fury tipped the pen, dipped it in boiling juices.   We were named a vicious interference against 'good and needful work,' 'defense of country,' 'legitimate scientific application,' and so on.

So far it was all predictable, a hatful of cliches and captivations.   Then came the shocker.   Mister Science concluded by declaring, to priests specifically, wayward sons of the Church mucking up his scene, that he was a practicing Catholic, who, on the day and hour suggested for our meeting, would be at Holy Mass. Presumably on behalf of our unregenerate selves. And not only on that day, he wrote, but every day. I bring up a disturbing matter (the daily worship, the daily crimes) in order to suggest a contrast to the lucid, sane, even memorable, letters in hand:

> When practically every public structure is morally askew, when scientists are whoring after Baal, when a culture is breaking up like dry sticks for the burning—at such a time, it is not to be thought wonderful that religion too should run with the harebrains. Forgetting as it runs. Running to forget.

A few must remember. Thank you, Reluctant Resister.

Daniel Berrigan, S.J.

This first edition of Reluctant Resister *has been printed on Plainwell's Natural Neutral, an acid-free sheet which meets the guidelines for permanence and durability of the Committee on Production Guidelines for Book Longevity of the Council on Library Resources. The type-face is* Plantin, *eleven point for the text, ten point for the introductory material. Designed by Alan Brilliant.*